Workshop Models for Family Life Education

EFFECTIVE STEPPARENTING

Jeffry H. Larson
James O. Anderson
Ann Morgan

Family Service America
44 East 23rd Street
New York, New York 10010

Copyright © 1984

Family Service America

44 East 23rd Street, New York, New York 10010

Library of Congress Cataloging in Publication Data

Larson, Jeffry H.
   Effective stepparenting

   (Workshop models for family life education)
   Bibliography: p.
   1. Stepparents--United States. 2. Parenting--United
States. I. Anderson, James O. II. Morgan, Ann,
1934-   . III. Title. IV. Series.
HQ759.92.L37 1984   646.7'8   84-8044
ISBN 0-87304-211-5

Printed in the U.S.A.

CONTENTS

FOREWORD

As the stepfamily continues to become a more prevalent family form in American society, the need for parenting programs specifically designed for stepparents will increase. The Effective Stepparenting Program (ESP) represents one of the first attempts to develop a parent education program specifically designed for parents in stepfamilies. It has undergone pilot tests in Lubbock, Texas, and in Dubuque, Iowa.

The manual is written for family life educators and family therapists who are particularly interested in stepparent education. Professionals who will find this manual most useful include marriage and family therapists, psychologists, parent educators, social workers, school counselors, and members of the clergy.

This manual is divided into six chapters. Chapter 1 introduces the stresses associated with being a stepparent and the resultant need for parenting programs for stepparents. Chapter 2 discusses the assumptions and principles underlying the ESP that are based on the stresses discussed in Chapter 1. Chapter 3 provides an overview of the sessions. In Chapters 4 and 5 respectively, we outline how to prepare to conduct a group and the group leader characteristics that facilitate the acquisition of knowledge and skills by the group participants. The eight group sessions are found in Chapter 6. Following the group sessions is information about a follow-up meeting and a bibliography.

Our goal is to assist stepparents and stepchildren to adjust to their new family system. Please evaluate each workshop session yourself as you have the group members evaluate them. We would sincerely appreciate your feedback on the program.

We express our gratitude to Dr. Nancy Bell and Dr. Judith Fischer of Texas Tech University for their suggestions and encouragement as this manual was developed. We also thank Glen Kuiper of Iowa State University for his support of this project. To Ruby Lindahl and Jeannie Larson, our typists, goes a special thank-you.

Jeffry H. Larson
James O. Anderson
Ann Morgan

PREFACE

<u>Workshop Models for Family Life Education</u> is a series of manuals intended to promote the exploration of new alternatives and the utilization of new options in day-to-day living through programs in family life education.

Basically, family life education (FLE) is a service of planned intervention that applies the dynamic process of group learning to improving the quality of individual and family living. The manuals are in workshop format and offer possible new approaches of service to families. They are meant to serve as a training mechanism and basic framework for group leaders involved in FLE workshops.

In 1974, the Family Service Association of America (FSAA) (Now Family Service America) appointed a National Task Force on Family Life Education, Development, and Enrichment. One of the goals of the task force was to assess the importance and future direction of family life education services within family service agencies. One of the recommendations of its report was to "recognize family life education, development, and enrichment as one of the three major services of the family service agency: family counseling, family life education, and family advocacy."[1] This recommendation was adopted by the Board of Directors of FSAA and has become basic policy of the association.

---

1. "Overview of Findings of the FSAA Task Force on Family Life Education, Development, and Enrichment," mimeographed (New York: Family Service Association of America, May 1976), p. 21.

An interest in family life education is a natural development of FSA's role in the strengthening of family life and complementary to the more traditional remedial functions of family agencies. FLE programs can add a new dimension to the services provided by family agencies. They can open an agency to the general population by providing programs which are appropriate for all families and individuals, not only for those at risk. They provide a new arena for service that deals with growth as well as dysfunction. They can encourage agencies to look beyond the therapeutic approach and to take on a new objective for the enrichment and strengthening of family life. For the participants, FLE programs can lead to increased understanding of normal stress, growth of esteem for one's self and others, development of communications skills, improved ability to cope with problem situations, development of problemsolving skills, and maximization of family and individual potential.

This series provides tangible evidence of FSA's continuing interest in family life education and of a belief in its future importance for family services. FLE programs, coordinated within a total agency program and viewed as a vital and integral part of the agency, can become key factors in family service concern for growth and development within all families.

Jeffry H. Larson is assistant professor of family relations, Montana State University, Bozeman; James O. Anderson directs a marriage and family therapy clinic in Lubbock, Texas; and Ann Morgan is assistant professor in the Psychology and Human Development Department, California Polytechnic State University, San Luis Obispo, California.

THE STRESSES OF STEPPARENTING

As the divorce rate has steadily increased in the United States in the last two decades, the number of individuals who remarry has also grown. About four out of every five of those who obtain a divorce will remarry. According to demographer Paul Glick, each year one-half million adults who remarry become stepparents to one or more children.[1] There may be close to 15 million children under the age of eighteen years living in stepfamilies. As this new family form continues to become more prevalent, it is important that professionals working with families become aware of the unique characteristics of the stepfamily.

Although the focus of this book is on stepparenting, it is important to note a statement by Esther Wald: "Two potential areas of stress and problems for the remarried family have been identified. First, this family has all the same growth and developmental problems that any other family has; second, it has additional problems that are rooted in the remarried family situation itself. These two major potential sources of problems combine to produce a lattice of inter-woven pressures and dilemmas."[2]

STRUCTURE OF STEPFAMILIES
John S. and Emily B. Visher compared the structure of stepfamilies to nuclear families, single-parent families, adoptive families, and

---

1. Paul C. Glick, "A Demographer Looks at American Families," Journal of Marriage and the Family 37 (1975): 15-26.
2. Esther Wald, The Remarried Family: Challenge and Promise (New York: Family Service Association of America, 1981), p. 14.

foster families and found stepfamilies and nuclear families to be
the least similar in six family patterns (see Table 1). Generally,
in stepfamilies, there is a biological parent living elsewhere and
the child is a member of more than one household, if the remarriage
followed a divorce. At least two persons in the newly reconstituted
family have sustained the loss of a spouse or parent. The relationship
between the biological parent and his or her child predates the marriage,
and the stepparent and the child are not legally related in most situations. Hence, a stepfamily differs significantly from a nuclear family
in terms of interpersonal relationships and perceptions. However,
stepfamilies are often treated as nuclear families by society and in
most cases, not understood.

The unique structure of stepfamilies leads to stress for family members.
Many adjustments must be made by both parents and children.

Sources of Stress
Dealing with Loss
The process of divorce and the transition to remarriage evoke an almost
universal feeling of loss and grief in both parents and children. When
the divorce finally takes place, even if the marriage has been miserable,
the parents experience the loss of a dream. The children are confronted
with a parental loss that they have not chosen. At the time of remarriage, the parent and particularly the children may still be grieving
their respective losses.

In addition, the children experience a second loss when their custodial
parent remarries, seemingly abandoning them. One study found that
the onset of problems for more than one-half of a group of stepchildren
was not at the time of divorce, but rather at the time of their parents'

2

TABLE 1. COMPARISON OF AMERICAN FAMILY PATTERNS - MAJOR STRUCTURAL CHARACTERISTICS*

Stepfamilies	Nuclear families	Single-parent families	Adoptive families	Foster families
Biological parent elsewhere		Biological parent elsewhere	Biological parent elsewhere	Biological parent elsewhere
Virtually all members have recently sustained a primary relationship loss		All members have recently sustained a primary relationship loss	The children have sustained a primary relationship loss	The children have sustained a primary relationship loss
An adult couple in the household	An adult couple in the household		Usually an adult couple in the household	Usually an adult couple in the household
Relationship between one adult (parent) and child predates the marriage			Relationship between one adult (parent) and child predates the marriage where stepchildren are adopted	
Children are members in more than one household		Children may be members in more than one household		Children may be members in more than one household
One adult (stepparent) not legally related to a child (stepchild)				The adults have no legal relationship to the child

*Emily B. Visher and John S. Visher, Stepfamilies: A Guide to Working with Stepparents and Stepchildren (New York: Brunner/Mazel, 1979). Used with permission.

3

remarriages.[3] Many children believe that they are not gaining another
parent but are being abandoned by their only remaining parent. Hence,
many children feel rejected. The new stepparent is faced with helping
the children deal with their loss and feelings of anger, guilt, rejection, and despair. This can be a great source of stress to stepparents
who enter remarriage believing the myth of "instant love"--that stepchildren will immediately love and appreciate them as their new parents.
Stepparents feel confused and disappointed when their stepchildren with-
draw from them. Unfortunately, most stepparents do not often have the
empathic listening skills that can help their stepchildren work through
their feelings.

Divided Loyalties

Children often experience a sense of divided loyalty toward their custodial parents and their new stepparents. A child may view the stepparent as an intruder and cling tenaciously to the custodial parent.
During the divorce period the children and the custodial parent are
both experiencing a loss and often enter into an exceptionally close
relationship. When remarriage occurs, the custodial parent or the
children may have difficulty "letting go." In addition, because the
new husband and wife do not easily have time alone together, he or she
may feel jealous of the attention the spouse gives to the children.
Thus, the stepparent is faced with both a spouse and stepchildren who
have their loyalties divided. The stress caused by this situation often
makes the stepparent feel jealous, resentful, and disappointed.

Ex-Spouses

Ex-spouses can create problems that are by definition related to the
first marriage. Studies have found that both spouses in a stepfamily

---

3. Annie M. White, "Factors Making for Difficulty in the Step-parent Relationship with Children," Smith College Studies in Social Work, vol. 14 (1943).

4

experience stress as a result of three major problems: (1) custody
and visitation difficulties; (2) children being upset by the ex-spouse's
telephone calls, broken promises, or late arrivals; and (3) competition
between current and ex-spouse. In addition, jealousy often results
if the stepparent's partner is preoccupied with "emotional garbage"
left over from his or her first marriage. These unresolved feelings
toward an ex-spouse often stir up anger and rivalry in the remarriage.

Role Confusion

Perhaps the greatest source of stress in stepparenting results from
the fact that the stepparent role is unclearly defined. The stepparent
is a newcomer--many times the intruder or interloper--to an established
family system. There is usually an attempt by any existing system to
expel a foreign body. Initially, because the stepparent is an intruder,
there may be an attempt, either overtly or covertly, to expel him or
her. This discomfort and upheaval may be the result of children not
knowing what to expect from the stepparent, since the role of the stepparent is ambiguous and ill-defined.

Because there are few models for a stepparent, it is a difficult task
to prepare for the role. There is no legally sanctioned role--the
stepparent-stepchild relationship confers no rights and imposes no duties.
Experiences and circumstances then reinforce the reality that the
stepparent is a "nonparent." This tends to erode the stepparent's sense
of authority and subsequently has a negative impact upon the stepparent-
stepchild relationship.

Discipline

Remarriage involving children, unlike a first marriage, brings with
it "instant parenthood." Sharing the parental role as an "instant parent"
is a major source of stress for stepparents. A problem faced by

stepparents as they try to share the parental role is the discipline of the children. Research studies stress the importance of discipline in the newly developed family. Effective discipline is a major key to the integration of the stepparent into the family. One of this manual's authors, Ann Morgan, questioned stepparents and their spouses on the subject of discipline problems and found that the explanations and examples given fell into six categories: (1) different methods of discipline; (2) the custodial parent's difficulty in sharing the role of disciplinarian with the stepparent; (3) the custodial parent's belief that the stepparent is picking on the child; (4) the child's refusal to obey the stepparent; (5) absence of children in the stepparent's prior marriage, and hence no prior parenting experience; and (6) a previous lack of discipline by the custodial parent during the single-parent period that spills over into the stepfamily situation.[4]

Many times the stepparent remains an outsider with regard to discipline while the custodial parent functions as sole authority figure in the family. This is due to the suddenness with which the stepparent is included in the family--a person with different ideas and a different set of feelings--and often creates tension and frequently severe discipline problems.

Questions of appropriate punishment are often the cause of family turmoil. Custodial parents are often defensive and may feel inadequate when stepparents criticize their children. As a result, matters of discipline are often left unresolved and the lines of authority remain unclear.

_____

4. Ann Morgan, "The Development of Stepfamilies: An Examination of Change Within the First Two Years" (Ph. D. diss., Texas State University, 1980).

6

Stepfathers may be "frozen out" of a parenting role in stepfamilies. In most families the father is the ultimate enforcer of discipline; he takes responsibility for limit setting and rule enforcing. Crucial to the resolution of the problem of "role freeze" in stepfamilies is awareness of the problem on the part of the custodial parent and a willingness to support the stepfather in his role as disciplinarian.

Stress often results as stepparents attempt to carve out a role in the stepfamily. At times they may feel defensive and inhibited by the knowledge that, in part, the success of the marriage depends on how successfully they are able to assume the parent role. On occasion, the fear of being seen as the "wicked stepparent" keeps the stepparent from being adequately assertive in discipline and moving into the parent role.

Summary

Stepparents have the unique and difficult task of developing roles and a workable family structure out of a tangle of new and old relationships. Attaining success amid the complexity and confusion of this network takes time. There is a period of adjustment stepfamilies go through in order to make the transitions to new family roles. This process is complicated by the fact that the roles are not clearly defined.

ADJUSTMENT IN STEPFAMILIES OVER TIME

A recent study of how stepfamilies adjust over time was conducted by Ann Morgan.[5] She studied the development of stepfamilies by examining changes within the first two years. She found that: (1) family cohesion,

---

5. Morgan, "The Development of Stepfamilies."

expressiveness, and satisfaction did not increase over the two-year period; and (2) the integration of the stepparent into decision making and discipline roles did not occur during the first two-year period. These findings are contrary to expectations based on previous research that satisfaction and unity would increase as time passed. She also found a tendency for stepparents to report greater satisfaction during the first six months of remarriage compared with seven to twelve and thirteen to twenty-four months. This seems to suggest that the first few months are divided into a "grace period" and a "jockeying for position period." Family members may be on their best behavior and overlook points of disagreement as the remarriage begins. If this is the case, pent-up frustrations and accumulated disagreements could lead to heightened stress following this "grace period."

It appears that stepparents face a number of stressful situations over a prolonged period of time. Especially apparent is their need for help in dealing with parenting issues and developing a viable role in the stepfamily. The adjustment problems faced by children and adults in stepfamilies and the heightened emotional climate that is produced suggest that stepparents are in great need of developing communication skills that will enable them to deal effectively with their own emotional responses and those of their stepchildren and spouse. Conflict is likely to be common in stepfamilies as spouses confront each other's different approaches to discipline and as visitation and ex-spouse problems arise. Hence, there is a need for stepparents to develop conflict-resolution or problem-solving skills.

The remainder of this chapter focuses on programs that have been developed to assist stepparents in the adjustment process and in the acquisition of communication, problem-solving, and other parenting skills.

Overview of Current Programs for Stepparents

At present, there is a great need for intervention strategies that can facilitate the adjustments adults and children need to make when they become a part of a stepfamily. Since parents and children in stepfamilies have separate adjustment needs and problems, intervention strategies should be aimed at both.

Few research-based intervention strategies have been developed to assist stepfamilies. Many authors emphasize the need for premarital counseling before remarriage. These programs involve group discussions of feelings about the first marriage and problems anticipated in the remarriage such as division of labor in the home, discipline, and visitation.

Some remarried couples attend group therapy. William Nichols, a family therapist, has conducted "Problems of a Second Marriage" groups.[6] Whereas some groups can be characterized as traditional group psychotherapy, Nichols's are more educational in nature. The Vishers have developed stepfamily "survival " discussion groups and communication training groups.[7] In the communication groups, four to six stepfamilies meet for ten hours on two consecutive days under the direction of two leaders. Adults and children meet together and then separate into a children's group and an adult's group so that topics of concern to each group can be discussed. The Stepfamily Association of America, created by the Vishers, conducts mutual help groups that consist of three to six couples who meet together on a weekly or bimonthly basis to share

6. William C. Nichols, "Today's Major Clinical Issue: The Remarried Family," Marriage and Divorce Today, 25 (1976): 445-49.
7. Emily B. and John S. Visher, Stepfamilies: A Guide to Working with Stepparents and Stepchildren (New York: Brunner/Mazel, 1979).

experiences and discuss their remarriages and stepfamily situations.
There is also an increasing number of "how-to" books and articles often
written by persons who have experienced stepparenting themselves.

The Effective Stepparenting Program (ESP) presented in this book is
a research-based educational program for stepparents and their spouses.
The program is based on stepparents' needs as identified in earlier
research studies of stepfamilies and in a more recent study by one of
the program authors, Ann Morgan.[8]   The ESP is a unique stepparenting
program in that it includes: (1) group discussions of the typical problems and issues faced by stepparents and stepchildren; (2) communication
and problem-solving skills training for stepparents and their spouses;
and (3) group discussions on discipline, the making of family rules,
and techniques for unifying the family. The ESP is based on the theory
that communication plays a vital role in the family system and that
it serves as a useful focus for intervention. This follows the theoret-
ical ideologies of family communication theorists Virginia Satir, Jay
Haley, and Don Jackson.

The ESP can be conducted as a four-session or as an eight-session program
consisting of two-hour sessions conducted one day a week for four or
eight consecutive weeks. To be effective, both the stepparent and his
or her spouse should attend. The sessions include: (1) the discussion
of issues and problems related to the stepparent role (for example,
relating to ex-spouses, divided loyalties, dealing with loss, establishing family unity and order); (2) discussion of typical adjustment
problems for stepchildren; and (3) the acquisition of three communication skills: effective listening, effective speaking, and effective

---

8. Morgan, "The Development of Stepfamilies."

10

problem solving. Homework assignments help motivate participants to
utilize the skills at home and hence, encourage generalization. In
addition, some sessions deal with specific parenting strategies that
are designed to help establish more order, trust, and cohesiveness in
the family and to give stepparents alternatives to the use of physical
punishment for discipline.

BASIC ASSUMPTIONS AND PRINCIPLES
OF THE EFFECTIVE STEPPARENTING PROGRAM

It is important that you, as group leader, understand and accept the general assumptions presented here about stepparenting, interpersonal communication, and family relationships before leading an ESP group. These assumptions are discussed below.

ASSUMPTIONS UNDERLYING THE ESP

1. Although stepfamilies are similar to natural or intact families, they have important structural and functional differences that require the development and use of educational materials specifically designed to meet their unique needs (see Chapter 1).

2. Stepparents need and want information about stepparenting and step-children in order to gain further insight into the unique problems and challenges of stepparenting.

3. Communication plays a vital role in the stepfamily system and it serves as a useful focus for intervention.

4. A complete and flexible repertoire of communication skills is more useful than a limited and rigid repertoire.

5. The ESP focuses on both the parent-child and the husband-wife relationship subsystems in the stepfamily system. The communication skills taught in the ESP are applied in both of these subsystems—participants are taught how to use the communication skills with both their children and their spouses.

6. Effective communication training for spouses in a stepfamily must include both spouses simultaneously and focus on their interaction with each other and with their children. This is important in order to create common perspectives and skills for changing interaction in directions as they choose. Research studies have shown that this kind of conjoint marriage and family intervention is superior to individual approaches.

7. The ESP focuses on equipping, not repairing. The ESP is not built around a therapy model designed to help partners solve a problem. Rather, the program is designed to equip people with the basic communication and problem-solving skills that will help them meet and deal more effectively with issues on their own.

8. The ESP focuses on the communication process, not on the content. By content we mean what partners talk about. Content is minimized in the ESP. Instead, the focus is on the communication process, increasing the couples' communication skills.

9. The ESP group is viewed as a helpful environment for learning as group members share common joys, sorrows, problems, and strategies that work in their relationships.

10. The use of homework assignments speeds progress and encourages generalization of the skills. The goal of the program is to teach participants skills that they can use in their daily lives, not just when they are in the group situation.

11. The ESP philosophy agrees with Bernard Guerney, founder of the Relationship Enhancement program, that the most expeditious approach to enhancing communication skills is to begin immediately: (1) teaching

participants what it is they need to know; (2) establishing appropriate life experiences--through practice in the group; (3) helping them perfect their skills--providing superivison; and (4) increasing the use of the skills in appropriate everyday life situations--through homework.[1]

12. Logistics are important. In preparing for a group meeting, the group leader needs a room that is conducive to developing an informal and relaxed atmosphere. This means careful selection of a room with good lighting, comfortable chairs, and temperature control. A group leader also needs such aids as a chalkboard or newsprint and an overhead projector.

---

1. Used by permission of Bernard Guerney.

OVERVIEW OF THE PROGRAM

This chapter provides a general overview of the eight ESP sessions and gives the rationale for the content of the sessions and the methods of instruction.

Four Sessions or Eight Sessions?

The ESP can be taught as either a four-week or an eight-week course. This program flexibility was built in to accommodate both group leaders and program participants.

The four-week format is most appropriate under these conditions:

1. The group members or leader are limited in the amount of time they can spend in the course.

2. The group leader is fairly inexperienced in conducting parent education courses--specifically courses involving the teaching of communication and problem-solving skills.

3. Group members want to learn about adjusting to stepparenting but do not care to devote the time and effort to develop all of the communication skills.

The eight-week format is most appropriate under these conditions:

1. The group members agree to devote eight weeks to the course.

2. The group leader has some experience in conducting parent education courses--specifically those involving the teaching of communication and problem-solving skills.

3. Group members agree to practice the skills in the group and at home.

It is also possible for the group leader to make an agreement with group members that after the fourth session they will decide if they want to continue with the second four sessions. This arrangement can clearly cause planning problems for a group leader and participants. The group leader may prefer to begin a large class that consists of both four-week participants and eight-week participants. After the first four weeks the group would then be reduced in size. Program leaders can develop any format they wish to based on their needs and experience and those of the participants.

The group session instructions are written for both experienced and inexperienced group leaders. It is assumed that in most cases only experienced group leaders will use sessions five through eight. Hence, the instructions for the first four sessions are more detailed and explicit than the instructions for the final four. Additional information for group leaders working with lower-income or lower-education stepparents is included at the end of each session.

In summary, the ESP is designed to allow a great deal of presentation flexibility. The authors believe that this flexibility will contribute to the program's applicability to a wide variety of group leaders, participants, and situations. A brief discussion of the contents of each session follows:

Session 1
The purposes of the first session are to help participants:
    Get acquainted and begin feeling comfortable in the group.
    Understand the structure and content of the program.

Set expectations for attendance at the weekly meetings and for homework completion.

Share with each other their common problems, worries, challenges, and joys of being a parent or stepparent in a stepfamily.

Voice their expectations of what they want to learn during the ESP.

Session 1 is basically a group experience that promotes the sharing of problems encountered in stepparenting. The group leader stimulates and encourages group discussion on topics such as the unique structural characteristics of stepfamilies, myths about stepfamilies, typical adjustment problems for stepchildren and stepparents, and the positive aspects of stepparenting. This sharing experience helps group members become better acquainted and feel more comfortable in the group. In addition, participants report that they do not "feel so bad" when they realize that others share their feelings and concerns. By voicing their expectations participants help the group leader set the agenda for future sessions.

Session 2

Session 2 and each successive session begins with a discussion of the homework assignment. This is done to reinforce the importance of doing the homework assignments and allow stepparents to ask questions or discuss problems they had with the homework. Stepparents who have completed the homework are positively reinforced by the leader; those who failed to complete the assignment are not chastised but rather encouraged to do the homework next time.

In Session 2 the group leader presents a short lecture to help initiate discussion on the issue of lack of clarity of the stepparent role in the area of discipline. This subject is addressed first because of its highest ranking as a problem by stepparents. Participants are also taught how to use natural and logical consequences with their stepchildren and how to develop family rules. These skills are seen as alternatives to physical punishment or other ineffective discipline methods.

Of the three communication skills taught to stepparents and their spouses in the ESP (listening, speaking, and problem solving), listening is discussed first. This procedure follows the observations of other interpersonal communication trainers that of the three skills, listening is usually the most challenging one for parents to learn. This session introduces parents to "effective listening" and allows them to begin practicing listening with close supervision by the group leader. Effective listening is the only communication skill worked on during the first four sessions. Participants who continue with the last four sessions develop effective speaking and effective problem-solving skills in addition to effective listening.

Session 3

The focus in this session is on typical adjustment problems of children in stepfamilies. These include dealing with loss, fantasies about the reunion of parents, loyalty issues, and so on. Stepparents are also taught how to facilitate the adjustment of children. The last half of Session 3 is spent sensitizing participants to barriers to effective communication and further developing their listening skills.

Session 4

Session 4 begins with a discussion of three typical problems for adults in stepfamilies: (1) financial concerns, for example, receiving and paying child support; (2) dealing with ex-spouses; and (3) visitation problems. In this session the group leader begins stressing the

18

importance of a healthy marital relationship to healthy parent-child relationships. The last half of this session is spent practicing effective listening.

Session 5

In this session and subsequent sessions, the emphasis is on communication skills practice. Participants are introduced to effective speaking skills and are given the entire session to practice.

Session 6

Participants are introduced to effective problem-solving skills in this session. Effective problem solving builds on the speaking and listening skills that the participants are developing. A portion of this session is also spent on learning how to conduct a family council. One of the purposes of the family council is to unify and bring order to the family. Stepparents, in particular, can gain from learning these skills since unity and order are often missing in stepfamilies (see chapter 1).

Session 7

This session begins with a discussion of the participants' homework assignment from the previous week--to conduct their first family council. This discussion provides an opportunity for the participants to express frustrations, joys, and surprise and allows the group leader to "troubleshoot." The remainder of this session is spent practicing problem solving.

Session 8

Session 8 is almost identical to Session 7. Additional components are a program summary, practice, and planning for future meetings. Participants also receive a book list and information about forming a stepparent organization.

PARTICIPANT WORKBOOKS

At the end of each group session in this manual are worksheets--exercises, role-play scripts, and evaluation forms--that are used in the sessions. Group members can obtain copies of these materials by purchasing the Participants Workbook. The workbook may be ordered from Family Service America. It is recommended that you request payment for the workbooks prior to the beginning of the group to allow enough time for delivery of the workbooks before the group begins.

Suggestions for Groups with Different Needs and Backgrounds

In the ESP sessions you will be aware that the examples given may not fit your group. You are encouraged to delete or change the examples where appropriate. For example, Session 3 talks about the child fantasizing a reunion between parents. This may not be as true of your group because of early desertion of the other parent or because of multiple marriages by many of the participants. Be aware of the needs and experiences of your group and adjust the sessions accordingly. Written homework assignments will be difficult for some groups. There may be a language problem, difficulty in completing a written assignment, or lack of motivation to "please" the instructor. Insistance on assiging homework may only contribute to lowered attendance as well as frustration for the leader when assignments are not completed. To avoid a confrontation over this issue, an alternate approach is suggested at the end of some sessions.

4
PREPARATION FOR A GROUP

RECRUITING[1]

No simple recruiting technique is likely to be successful by itself.
The methods you choose will depend on you, the organization or agency
you are connected with, the available resources, and how well you are
known in the community. The best approach is to use a combination
of as many techniques as possible. Listed below are a number of techniques that you might include in your overall plan.

If you are affiliated with an agency or organization (for example,
a social service agency) you will probably find a large number of
stepparents among the groups of people you serve. These poeple are
ready recruits and can serve as scouts for you in locating other prospective participants.

What promotion strategies can you use? Mailings of brochures and
advertisements in newspapers are only effective if you can provide
follow up. Using these techniques alone will reap few participants.
If you use brochures or advertisements (which can be expensive), following them with 30-second radio announcements (public service announcements) and trying to get the local television station to interview
you on "this new parenting program," may prove a successful way to
reach prospective group members. Telephone clergymen, social service
agency workers, doctors, and other related professional people and
inform them of the benefits of the program to stepparents with whom

---

1. Sherod Miller, E. W. Nunnally, and D. B. Wackman, Couple Communication Instructor Manual (Minneapolis, Minn.: Interpersonal Communication
Programs, Inc., 1977). Used by permission.

they associate. Most newspapers print public service meetings in a special section. Have the program announced and include your name and phone number for people who have some interest but want to know more.

You can also focus on an organization with membership or clientele that has some likelihood of interest in the program. Many congregations, for example, have an interest in family life education but do not have the personnel to offer the programs. By working with their leaders you may be able to establish yourself as a consultant and offer the ESP to the members of the congregation. The same process will often work with social service agencies (for example, community mental health, family service) that welcome some assistance with preventative family life education.

School systems through adult education programs and community colleges are also natural contacts for the program. In some communities the ESP could be offered through extension classes with one or both spouses receiving credit.

In making contacts with organizations, it is important that you work with the organization to reach the people they serve. This generally requires support by those who run the organization. When the contact is made, try to gain some active support from the person in charge. Ask for an opportunity to speak directly to members of the organization, or to make information about the ESP available to members through posters, brochures, and announcements in the organization's bulletin.

CONTRACTS
One of the most disappointing things that can happen to a group leader is to have the size of his or her group steadily dwindle as the weeks

22

go by. This situation is common to many interpersonal skills training programs. An essential feature in the success of your group is a viable contract with each couple prior to the first group session. The contract is an agreement between the couple and you which indicates that they understand the purposes, expectations, and structure of the ESP and that both spouses want to involve themselves in understanding the material and practicing the skills presented in the program.

A preprogram meeting (usually about twenty minutes) is extremely valuable. It gives each couple a chance to establish some rapport privately with you by asking questions, clarifying expectations, and dealing with any special concerns. Besides preparing parents to participate in the program, this preprogram meeting reduces the drop-out rate. Whenever leaders have problems conducting a group, the roots of the problem usually go back to the contract, that is, no contract was made, expectations were not set, or concerns were not effectively dealt with.

Contracts are based on an important learning principle: Better learning occurs when a person is highly involved in his or her learning experience. Therefore, the contract is an integral part of the ESP.

In addition to assuring an understanding of the objectives and format of the program, the establishment of a contract motivates each person to make his or her own choices and take responsibility for his or her own learning. This minimizes the likelihood of a spouse enrolling in the program to placate the other, or enrolling with the expectation of being entertained.

The contract discussion is not a "screening interview" to decide who is "fit" or who is "unfit" to participate in the ESP. Rather, the discussion is designed to give each spouse the opportunity to acquaint himself or herself with the ESP and ask any questions--and then to personally decide whether to enroll in the group. The meeting also gives you the chance to determine if the objectives of the program are understood and that they match with the desires of the participants.

Contract Outline

Below is an outline of the content of the basic contract between a group leader and a couple.

1. Discuss the goals and general format of the program (see Chapters 1 and 3 for a review of the goals and format). Be sure to stress that the ESP focuses on teaching practical communication skills for dealing effectively with day-to-day issues.
2. Go over the expectation for participation.
    a. Attendance at all sessions.
    b. Practice and experimentation with communication skills in the group and at home.
3. Assure participants that they always have a choice about when they talk and what they talk about in front of the group.
4. Go over the logistics--dates, time, location, informal dress, fees, and so on.

Sometimes, it may be impossible to conduct the contract interview in person. In these cases, you may have to do the contract over the telephone or in writing. In such instances, you should ensure that you communicate with both spouses, not just with the spouse who made the initial contact.

5
GROUP STRUCTURE AND LEADER CHARACTERISTICS

The optimal size of a group and the length of the meetings are inter-
related factors. The smaller the group, the more time each person
has to practice the communication and problem-solving skills under
supervision. A group of six-to-eight participants (three or four
couples) is the ideal size for an eight-session group. A four-session
group may include more members. Group meetings last two hours, once
a week for either a four- or eight-week period. The group can meet
in any suitable room--preferably one with a chalk board, a screen for
the use of overhead transparencies, comfortable chairs, good lighting,
and a comfortable temperature. Careful attention by you to these room
variables will help the participants in the learning process.

If resources permit, it is desirable to have two group leaders and
ideal to have a male and female as coleaders. This arrangement gives
the male and female participants same-sex role models and a person
of their own sex whom they may believe can empathize more easily with
their point of view. However, it is not a serious handicap to run
a group alone.

The ESP sessions are systematic and the instructions to group leaders
are specific. Some previous experience with conducting parent education
groups is desirable for those conducting four-session programs. To
conduct an eight-session program a group leader should have past experience conducting parent education or marriage enrichment groups (for
example, Parent Effectiveness Training, Couples Communication, Relationship Enhancement). In addition, group leaders conducting eight-
session workshops should have a good understanding of Rogerian
techniques of counseling and the techniques of behavioral reinforcement.

LEADER CHARACTERISTICS

To be a successful leader of the ESP one should be an innovative and dedicated teacher and a skilled social reinforcer. A discussion of what these roles are follows below.

The ESP Leader as Teacher

The ability to teach effectively is learned. Some ESP leaders already have teaching skills, some develop the skills as they teach the ESP. A group leader with highly developed teaching skills usually insures that the ESP will be a successful experience for the participants. The purpose of this section is not to teach you how to teach but rather to make suggestions that will help the group participants learn more efficiently. When leading an ESP group, it is important to remember these teaching guidelines:

1. Be enthusiastic and confident. Avoid statements like: "This is the first time I have ever led a group, so please excuse my nervousness" or "Boy, am I tired tonight." These kinds of statements discourage people and make them think that this group is not very important to you.

2. Make sure the room is ready before the group meets. A leader who appears ready and enthusiastic when the participants arrive will instill enthusiasm in the group members which is especially important if people meet in the evening after a long day at work.

3. Allow time for questions. Answer as many questions as possible, but admit it when you do not know an answer. Try to find the answer between sessions or refer the participant to a resource.

26

4. Know the material. You should know and understand the material well enough to avoid using extensive notes. Discuss the material with the group members; do not read or lecture to them.

5. Use as many visual and auditory aids as possible. People learn more efficiently and retain information longer if they receive it through more than one of the senses. Talk to the group (auditory) and show them examples (visual) simultaneously. Use a chalk board, overhead projectors, and handouts as much as possible.

6. Be a part of the group, sit with it; do not "stand before them" behind a podium. Use personal examples (as appropriate) of the use of the principles and skills taught in the course.

The ESP Leader as a Social Reinforcer

The ESP uses a modified version of the training methodology of Bernard Guerney when teaching group members communication skills.[1] Participants are trained by the group leader through the use of social reinforcement. The term social reinforcement refers to use of statements such as : "fine, good, right, very good, excellent, great, terrific, wonderful, beautiful, you're doing very well, and that was excellent for a first attempt."

According to Guerney:

> Such responses are appropriate whenever a group member: (1) responds well; (2) responds at a level better than his/her general level has been; (3) corrects or improves his/her own

---

1. Used by permission of Bernard Guerney.

response; or (4) follows an appropriate suggestion made by the group leader. These kinds of social reinforcers should be made as frequently as possible during the initial, didactic phases of training. Once participants are performing at a consistently high level, they are no longer necessary on such a frequent basis but should still be employed whenever a person has come up with a well-formed response.[2]

Nonverbal reinforcement includes nodding your head and other gestures that commonly are used to indicate approval. Nonverbal reinforcement is particularly useful because it can be used frequently without interfering with the flow of conversation.

In order to permit the use of nonverbal cues, it is desirable for you to sit so that you can be seen in the peripheral vision of the participants who are practicing the skills (see Figure 1). Sit a bit back from and equal distance from each participant. This arrangement allows you to provide touch cues (for example, a pat on the back) and hand and facial gestures for each person.

Figure 1. Seating Arrangement for Skills Practice

_____

2. Ibid.

6
GROUP SESSIONS

The eight ESP group sessions follow. Each session is arranged as follows:

1. Group agenda for the session
2. Worksheets, exercises, role play scripts
3. Evaluation form

Note that each session lasts for two hours with a ten-minute break in the middle of each session. The recommended amount of time you spend in each part of a session is printed in the lefthand margin. Remember that this is only a recommendation--do not hurry to the next part of the session if the group is interested in further discussion of the current topic.

SESSION 1

I. INTRODUCTION

OBJECTIVES: Group members get to know each other. Establish group closeness through sharing of common family situations.

A. When participants arrive, give them the registration forms to complete, numbered 1A in the Participant Workbook. This provides data that will be useful to you as the program progresses.

B. As group leader, you should strive to establish a relaxed and comfortable atmosphere from the very beginning. Small talk about parking, child care, and so on can help in this regard. Humor, if compatible with your style, can be very effective as well.

C. Provide name tags for participants.

10 min. D. Welcome the participants and begin the following get-acquainted exercise. After introducing yourself, an introduction to the workshop might be: "We're glad you're here to take part in the Effective Stepparenting Program. The first thing we would like to do is begin getting acquainted with one another. Please pair off with someone you don't know, introduce yourself, and tell a little about your stepfamily situation--things such as how long you have been married, the number and ages of your children. In a few minutes, I'll ask you to introduce the person you have been talking to and tell a little about that person and his or her family. I think that you will find that as a group you have a good many things in common."

10   E. Provide each person with an opportunity to introduce the other
min.   person of their pair to the group.

II. PROGRAM OVERVIEW

10   OBJECTIVE: Establish expectations for the program.
min. It is important that you provide a brief overview of the program
to let the participants know what to expect from the program.
The following outline provides the main points to be covered and
statements that you might make. These statements are provided
only as examples, and you are urged to adapt the main points to
your own personality and style of communication.

    A. <u>Goals of the program</u>
        1. Provide information about adjustment in stepfamilies
            a. Adjustment of children
            b. Adjustment of adults
        2. Facilitate the development of skills that participants
            can use in working out their own adjustment problems
            a. Listening skills
            b. Speaking skills
            c. Problem-solving skills
            d. Organizing skills

Stress that the communication skills that will be taught in this
course (listening, speaking, and problem-solving) are to be used
with both children and spouse. Participants will have an opportunity to practice with their children and their spouse. The
philosophy of this program stresses that the marital relationship
has a significant effect upon the quality of the parent-child

relationship. Research has shown that there is a strong relation-ship between marital adjustment and family environment.

Stress that the program consists of two parts: Part 1, the first four sessions, consists of: group discussions of typical problems and strengths in stepfamilies, including adult adjustment problems and child adjustment problems; and learning and practicing how to be a more effective listener. Part 2, sessions five through eight, includes learning and practicing the following additional skills: effective speaking, effective problem solving, and family organization techniques. Participants should already know this information as a result of their previous discussion with you and contract to participate. Be sure to clear up any questions or doubts that people may have.

Suggested Group Leader Statements

"I would like to give you a brief overview of the program so you'll know what to expect tonight and in the coming weeks. This will be an educational experience. It is not marriage or family counseling. During the first four weeks, I will be providing some information re-garding the adjustment processes in stepfamilies, looking at the adjust-ment of children as well as adults. I will also teach you how to be better listeners, which will help you and your children adjust to the stepfamily situation.

"During the second four weeks of the program I will further refine your listening skills, teach you speaking skills, problem-solving skills, and family organization skills. In summary, the first four sessions are primarily group discussions, sharing information, and learning one skill--listening. The last four sessions include group discussions, but focus on teaching you listening, speaking, and problem-solving and organizing skills. The nature of these skills will become apparent as we move through the program."

    B.   Program Schedule and Format

        1. One meeting per week for eight weeks with each session lasting about two hours.

            a.   Promptness in arriving on time is vital

            b.   Attendance at each session is very important

            c.   Participants should bring their Participant Workbooks to each session

        2. Each session will follow basically the same pattern: Review of homework assignments, presentation of information, a break, and the development of skills. An alternate approach to several sections is included at the end of the session for leaders with groups with special needs. For example, when the term homework assignment and the expectation of completion of assignments create problems or are met with resistance, an alternate approach is suggested.

Suggested Group Leader Statements

"Let me say something about our schedule, the format of the sessions, and some things you can do to help us make our meetings most helpful to everyone. We will meet on Tuesday evenings (or whatever evening has been arranged for earlier) from 7:30-9:30. Tonight is the first of eight sessions, so we will be meeting each Tuesday evening for the next seven weeks. We are planning to start on time each week and I hope you will make a special effort to be here promptly at 7:30. Since each session builds upon the previous session, it is very important that you attend every session. If something major comes up and you can't make a session, we will try to work with you to get you caught

up on what you missed; however, we're hoping everyone will arrange
to be here for each session.

"We will be following this pattern in each of the sessions: Each session
will begin by us talking about the homework assignment from the previous
week. Some homework involves reading from your workbook, other homework
requires that you try a new skill. The homework discussion will be
followed by a presentation of information about stepfamilies and group
discussion. Then we will take a short break. Following the break,
we will learn a specific skill that you can put to use in your families.
In closing, a homework assignment will be given for the following week.

"I have mentioned homework assignments a couple of times. Let me explain
what I mean. First, I believe that what happens in our group meetings
is only a small part of what is required to make this program really
helpful to you. I would like you to incorporate the information and
skills you learn during the weekly meetings in your daily family lives.
How you do that, of course, is up to you. I will be making some
assignments each week to suggest how you can make some applications
of what you are learning in the group meetings.

"Do you have questions?"

III. The Stepfamily Phenomena

OBJECTIVE: To help stepparents feel more comfortable in their
stepfamily situation by sharing of common problems, challenges,
and strengths.

20
min.
This part of session 1 is a leader-guided group discussion of what
it is like to be a stepparent, to be married to a stepparent, and

34

to have stepchildren and biological children in the same household. The emphasis here is on self-disclosure by participants on the topics listed below. Participants should be given the opportunity to share their problems, fears, challenges, questions, doubts, and joys. This process accomplishes two things: stepparents learn that others share their same problems, doubts--they learn that their situation is not unique, and participants become better acquainted, begin to feel more comfortable in the group, and develop more enthusiasm about the course and its applicability to their lives.

Listed below are the topics to be discussed. Following each topic is information that you can introduce into the group discussion to enrich it or as a stimulant for more discussion.

A. <u>Definition and Incidence of Stepfamilies</u>

Begin the discussion by asking one or more of the following questions:

1. "What is a stepfamily?

"Definition of a stepfamily: A family in which one or both partners have been previously married. Stepfamilies are also called reconstituted, remarried, and blended, or reorganized families."

2. "How common are stepfamilies?

"One-half million adults and one million children become a part of stepfamilies each year. There are six million children under eighteen years of age living in step-families."

3. "What are some unique characteristics of stepfamilies?

"Prior to the 1900s most stepfamilies were the result of the death of a spouse, few resulted from divorce. With the increase in the number of divorces, today, 80

percent of the stepchildren in this country are children
of divorce. So, we have a new family pattern emerging
that is unique in a lot of ways:

>Frequently one of a child's biological parents lives
>in a different household.
>Children are often members of more than one household.
>There is no legal relationship between stepparent and
>stepchildren.
>Ask the group to suggest other ways in which stepfamilies
>are unique.

The uniqueness of stepfamilies means that parents and children in stepfamilies have some special needs which must
be met if adjustment is to occur."

4. "What are some of the widespread misconceptions or myths
about stepfamilies or stepparents which can hamper adjustment?
"The wicked stepmother. This myth is seen best in children's
stories such as Cinderella, Snow White, and Hansel and
Gretel. This myth often places unnecessary strain on mothers
as they assume a stepmother role.
"Instant love. According to this myth, stepparents and
stepchildren in any given family should instantly and
naturally love one another. This is very unrealistic,
but such expectations can prompt people to judge themselves
a failure in blending two families.
"Make up to the children. Stepparents are usually aware
of the emotional trauma stepchildren have suffered as a
result of their parents' divorce. There is a tendency
to try to compensate the children for this hurt. This
is particularly true of stepmothers. They may attempt
to be overly warm and loving and give a lot to the
stepchildren. Problems can arise from this when the

husbands begin to feel deprived or left out. The stepchildren may view this extra attention as an attempt to
replace their natural mothers. It is not possible to
take away or make up for past pain.

"A stepfamily can be molded into a nuclear family. Some
stepparents expect that their new family will eventually
have the same characteristics, cohesiveness, and stability
as a nuclear family. They fail to realize that the stepfamily is significantly different from the nuclear family,
and the development of warmth, cohesiveness, and stability
will take more time and patience."

10
min.
BREAK

B. Typical Adjustment Problems Faced by Children in Stepfamilies
1. "What are some of the typical loyalty problems children
face when their parent remarries? Divided loyalties. It is
common for children in stepfamilies to feel torn in the relationship between their biological parent and their stepparent.
Acceptance of the stepparent seems like disloyalty to the
biological parent, so children freqeuntly resist showing approval and acceptance of their new stepparent. The stepparent
is often compared unfavorably with the natural parent and this
may come out in statements such as, 'My dad never missed when
he shot baskets with me' or 'My real mother really knows how
to cook brownies.'"
2. "What problems are encountered when children become a
part of two households: biological and stepparent homes?
Being part of two households is another issue frequently faced
by children in stepfamilies. They may spend weekends or
vacations with their other biological parent and his or her

new spouse. The two households may function very differently from each other and the child may experience adjustment difficulties moving back and forth between two households. It is not uncommon for a child to return home after visiting his or her other parent and compare the two places unfavorably, such as, Dad always lets me stay up to watch the late movie. I can't do anything around here."

3. "Is it typical for stepchildren to _not_ love their new stepparent? Another adjustment issue involves the myth of instant love. Youngsters recognize that they are expected to love their stepparent. But love relationships take time to develop. When they don't feel warmth toward their stepparent they may feel pressure to deny their own feelings or may feel guilty for not feeling more affectionate toward their stepparent."

4. "Why is it difficult for a stepchild to accept discipline from a stepparent? An adjustment frequently faced by children in stepfamilies involves accepting discipline from their stepparent. I don't have to do what you say, you're not my _real_ Dad (or Mom), is a commonly heard statement in many stepfamilies. Children or youngsters may also play one parent against the other. For example, if the stepparent administers some form of discipline, the child will run to his or her biological parent and try to win sympathy. Children are adept at driving wedges between their parents in this way."

C. "I would like to emphasize in concluding this section of the program that having to make adjustments in stepfamilies can be a very positive experience for children. It can teach them flexibility, how to work out and develop relationships with other people, and generally prepare them for adulthood. There's no

need for parents to try to shield their children from adjustments, the need is for parents to help children learn to make
adjustments as well as possible."

IV. STEPPARENTING: THE POSITIVE ASPECTS

OBJECTIVE: To assist stepparents in becoming more aware of the
positive aspects of stepparenting and to encourage them in the
adjustment process.

15
min.

A. Ask each participant to spend the next five minutes thinking
about the positive aspects of being a stepparent and having stepchildren.

"We have been discussing some of the issues, challenges, myths,
and problems related to stepfamilies. There are also many joys,
strengths, and benefits from being in a stepfamily. We want to
discuss those now. Each of you move your chair to a place in the
room where you will have some privacy. Spend the next five
minutes listing as many positive aspects of being in a stepfamily
as you can think of." Distribute pencils and have participants
turn to handout 1B of their workbooks.

B. Spend the remaining fifteen minutes having participants share
the positive aspects of being in a stepfamily.

V. HOMEWORK

5
min.

A. Ask group members to think about the typical problems stepparents have in adjusting to stepchildren. Stress that you
want them to particularly think about the role they play as

"another parent" to a child. Ask them to think about problems
they have had in the area of discipline.

B. Ask each couple to spend twenty minutes discussing the
discipline being carried out in their home. What do they <u>think</u>
about it? How do they <u>feel</u> about it? What would they like to
see changed? Tell them that the group will discuss discipline
next week.

VI. EVALUATION OF SESSION 1

Have each participant complete the Session 1 evaluation form numbered
1C in their workbooks.

<u>Alternative Group Leader Statement for Section II,B and Homework</u>
"We will be following this pattern in each of the sessions: Each
session will begin by talking about the activities that you have done
since the last session. That will be followed by my presenting some
information about stepfamilies and providing you with an opportunity
to discuss that information. Then we will take a short break.
Following the break, we will learn a specific skill that you can put
to use in your families. In closing, I will make suggestions about
activities you can do at home or skills you can practice during the
week.

"I have mentioned the practicing of the skills at home and other
activities that you can do between sessions. Let me talk a little more
about that. First, I believe that what happens in our group meetings
is only a small part of what is required to make this program really
helpful to you. I would like you to incorporate the information and

skills you learn during the weekly meetings in your daily family living. How you do that, of course, is up to you. I will be making some suggestions each week to help you apply what you are learning in the session."

Homework

Stress the importance of continuing the discussion of discipline at home. For example, you might say: "Next week, set aside some time for the two of you, fifteen to twenty minutes, to discuss discipline in your home. How satisfied are you with the way discipline is handled? How you _feel_ about it? What changes you would like to see?" It is a good idea to write your expectations on the chalkboard or have it written on a flipchart, so that you can stress the three parts of the "assignment."

1A--THE EFFECTIVE STEPPARENTING PROGRAM
INFORMATION SHEET

1. Your names: Husband: _____

    Wife: _____

2. Your ages: Husband: _____

    Wife: _____

3. Your home address: _____

    _____

4. Phone numbers: Work place: _____ Home: _____

5. Month and year of your remarriage: _____

6. Your occupations: Husband: _____

    Wife: _____

7. Your highest educational attainments: Husband: _____

    Wife: _____

8. Names and ages of children living with you:

    a. Husband's children by previous marriage: _____

    _____

    b. Wife's children by previous marriage: _____

    _____

    c. Children born in current marriage: _____

    _____

1B--Stepparenting: The Positive Aspects

List below the advantages and positive things about being a stepparent or having a spouse who is a stepparent. List at least ten positive things.

1.

2.

3.

4.

5.

6.

7.

8.

9.

10.

More? List:

Session 1 Worksheet

1C--Evaluation of Session One

Please rate the following items according to how helpful you think they are or will be to you in your stepfamily situation:

1 = Very helpful

2 = Helpful

3 = Unhelpful

4 = Very unhelpful

_____   1.   Discussion of the prevalence and uniqueness of stepfamilies.

_____   2.   Discussion of the myths regarding stepfamilies (for example, the wicked stepmother myth).

_____   3.   Discussion of the adjustment issues faced by children in stepfamilies (for example, divided loyalties, being a part of two households, lack of love for stepparent, accepting discipline).

What was most helpful in this session?

What was least helpful in this session?

How could this session have been more helpful to you?

SESSION 2

I. DISCUSS HOMEWORK

OBJECTIVE: To encourage homework completion by asking for feedback and questions.

10
min.

A. Ask participants if they have any questions or comments about last week's session.

B. Ask participants what kinds of adjustment problems they have had as they have tried to "carve out" the role of stepparent. Ask them what problems they have had with discipline.

II. ADJUSTMENT ISSUES FACED BY ADULTS IN STEPFAMILIES

OBJECTIVES: To establish group closeness and allow for catharsis on common issues and problems for stepparents. To help participants begin to define their roles as parents and stepparents. To help participants learn a new discipline skill.

Present this section following a lecture and discussion format. To provide a link between this session and the first you might say,

"During the last session we looked at some of the adjustment issues faced by children in stepfamilies. Tonight's session will focus attention on some of the adjustment issues faced by parents in stepfamilies."

This opening provides a lead into the lecture and discussion on the lack of clarity regarding role expectations.

45

5
min.

A. Lack of Clarity Regarding Role Expectations

Begin by asking the participants how they learned how to be stepparents. This draws attention to the fact that most stepparents
have not learned their role from their own parents. Point out
that society has not yet developed roles for stepparents.

"Most stepparents have received little or no direction regarding
how they are to function in their new families. As a result, they
often enter the stepfamily uncertain about how they should relate
to other family members.

"It is very common for stepparents to have unrealistic expectations regarding their roles and then experience a sense of failure
at not being able to live up to those expectations. For example,
a stepfather may envision himself providing instant nurture and
support for his stepchildren whom he assumes have experienced a
great deal of hurt, but quickly finds that they don't even want
to be near him.

"Television models support unrealistic expectations of parents in
stepfamilies. Television often portrays stepparents with the
wisdom of Solomon and the patience of Job, therefore, all of the
family problems are solved in thirty minutes.

"One area in particular in which roles are not clearly spelled out
in stepfamilies is that of discipline."

10
min.

B. Dealing with Discipline

"Discipline is an important key to a stepfamily becoming unified.
A unified family is one in which: (1) there is a set of norms;
(2) each person has status within the group; (3) people in the

46

family feel attached to it as a unit; and (4) there is a clear idea about who is in the family and who is not. Developing into an integrated stepfamily may take from one and one-half to two years or even longer.

"It is vital for parents to reach agreement about discipline early in the development of their family. Children are quick to sense differences in their parents' views and will play one parent against the other. Another difficulty that often arises involves the biological parent undermining the stepparent's efforts to discipline the children. The biological parent may want the step-parent to discipline his or her children. However, when the stepparent does exercise discipline, the biological parent may rush to the defense of the children. This conflict leaves the stepparent confused regarding his or her role in disciplining the children and he or she may cease enforcing any discipline. The biological parent may interpret this withdrawal as a lack of interest, and the children are inadvertently encouraged to resist discipline from their stepparent. It is important for parents and stepparents in stepfamilies to reach an agreement regarding how and by whom discipline will be administered in their family.

"In most families it is best for the biological parent and the stepparent to share the authority figure position in the family. Stepparents have a right to discipline children in their family. Other people are not real parents (policemen, teachers, for example) but they exercise authority over children in their care. The age of the children may influence how quickly and smoothly the stepparent can assume a place of authority in the family. Generally, the younger the children are the easier it is for the stepparent to assume a place of authority.

"In order for the natural parent and the stepparent to share authority in the family and be united in their discipline of the children, they need to discuss and reach agreement about several concerns:

Specific behaviors that are acceptable or unacceptable to each person

Methods of discipline: time-out, loss of privileges, physical punishment

Who is responsible for discipline and under what conditions."

As group leader you should repeatedly summarize sections of material and develop transitions into new sections. For example:

"We have considered the importance of discipline in bringing about integration in a stepfamily and the importance of the biological parent and the stepparent being united in disciplining their children. I am now going to introduce some disciplinary techniques that I hope you will be able to use. First we will consider natural and logical consequences, and then I will suggest some guidelines for making family rules."

20 min.

C. Natural and Logical Consequences

1. "Using natural and logical consequences teaches a child to be responsible for his or her own behavior. In using natural consequences the parent stays out of the way of nature and the child learns from the results of his or her own behavior.

"For example, take an eight-year-old son, who is almost late for school every day because he gets up too late and then dawdles along. You have to constantly nag him to get him

48

going. Using natural and logical consequences you could give him an alarm clock and show him how to use it. Tell him that you expect him to be responsible for getting up, dressed, fed, and out of the door to school. If he misses breakfast, permit the natural consequences of hunger to bring about a decision, to allow time for breakfast next time. If he is late to school, let him experience the natural consequences from the teacher. You may want to tell the teacher what you are trying to accomplish and get his or her cooperation.

"In using logical consequences, the parent plans the consequences that are logically related to the child's misbehavior. For example, if your son gets his shoes muddy, he cleans them up before entering the house. Or, your daughter spills something, so she cleans it up before leaving the table."

2. After briefly describing the use of consequences as described above, give the participants an opportunity to identify consequences in various situations. Present the situations below and let participants take turns formulating a consequence. It is important that you do not put unnecessary strain on the participants. If one person is having difficulty identifying a consequence, go on to the next person. Below are some possible situations and consequences. You may want to develop your own list or add to this list as well.

"I have explained natural and logical consequences and now I would like you to practice formulating consequences for several misbehaviors. I'll go around the room asking each of you to suggest a consequence."

Misbehavior	Natural or Logical Consequence
Child is helping you prepare for supper and leaves some kitchen chore unfinished.	Delay the meal until the chore is completed.
Dirty clothes are left in a pile in the closet.	Wash the clothes only when they are placed in the clothes hamper.
Child accidentally spills milk at dinner table.	Have the child clean up the mess before finishing his or her meal.
Child forgets to take lunch money to school.	Let the child work out the difficulty at school as best he or she can. Don't assume responsibility for the child's forgetfulness.
Child continues leaving his or her bicycle in the driveway.	Restrict the child's use of bicycle for a designated period of time and then let the child try again to keep the bicycle in its proper place.

3. "It is important to know how to apply natural and logical consequences. These guidelines should be followed, please look

at 'Guidelines for Using Consequences' numbered 2A in your workbooks.[1]

"Provide choices. Examples of choices phrased in a respectful manner are: 'Michelle, we're trying to watch television. You may settle down and watch the program with us or leave the room. You decide which you'd rather do'. Or, 'If you plan to go outside after school, you'll need to change your clothes'. The choice is obvious. To state the alternate choice would be unnecessary. Some logical consequences involve stating your intentions and letting the child decide how to respond: 'I'm willing to wash only what is in the hamper'.

"As you follow through with a consequence, give the children assurance that there will be an opportunity to change the decision later. This encourages children. For example: Mother, following through matter-of-factly: 'I see you have decided to leave the room. Feel free to come back when you are ready to settle down'. Or, Father (following through matter-of-factly): 'I see you haven't changed your clothes like I asked you to, so I assume you have decided to stay in today and try again tomorrow'.

"If the misbehavior is repeated, extend the time that must elapse before the child may try again. 'I see that you're

_____

1. "Adapted from Systematic Training for Effective Parenting (STEP): Parent's Handbook. Copyright 1976, by Don Dinkmeyer and Gary McKay. Published by American Guidance Service, Publishers' Building, Circle Pines, MN 55014."

still not ready to settle down and have decided to leave the room. You may try again tomorrow night'. <u>Or</u>: 'Because you went outside again without changing your clothes first, you will have to stay in for the next two days. Then you can try again'."

"To make sure your action is not punishment, but an expression of logical consequences:
Show an 'open' attitude: give the child a choice and accept the child's decision.
Use a friendly tone of voice that expresses good will.
Make sure the consequence is logically related to the mis-behavior."

15
min.

D. <u>Making Family Rules</u>
"We have just discussed using consequences to help children learn to be responsible for their own behavior. Rules are closely related to the idea of consequences. Families tend to be more organized, efficient, and happy if family rules are fair and firm. Everyone in the family should have a say in the rules that are made. This participation in the rule making helps motivate each person to follow the rules. We are now going to talk about how to make family rules." Use an overhead projector and/or have group members turn to "Guidelines for Making Rules" numbered 2B in their workbooks. Present the following:

1. "Children learn to do what is reinforced. Rules help children learn what they are supposed to do and when it is supposed to be done. The long-range plan of parents is to help their children learn to guide their own behavior and make good decisions. Children need to be taught rules for

living with others, how to be cooperative, responsible, and so on. By spelling out rules for the children, parents are able to know when to reinforce, to ignore, or apply consequences to their children. Rules help parents to be consistent in training their children. Rules also help the child remember what is expected of him or her."

2. Guidelines for Making Rules[2]

a. Where possible, rules should be short, stated positively, and easy to remember.

THIS WAY	NOT THIS WAY
Homework before television.	If you don't get your homework done, you can't watch television.
Wash hands before eating.	You can't eat unless you wash your hands.

b. Rules should specify a behavior and a consequence.

THIS WAY	NOT THIS WAY
You make your bed before breakfast.	Make your bed each morning.
Dishes must be washed before you can watch television.	Dishes must be washed each night.
Clean your room on Saturday before going out to play.	Clean your room each Saturday.

c. Rules should be stated so that they can be easily enforced.

(1) It should be easy to know whether the rule was followed or not.

---

2. Wesley Becker, Parents Are Teachers (Champaign, Ill.: Research Press, 1971), p. 148. Used by permission.

THIS WAY	NOT THIS WAY
You must wash your hands and face, comb your hair, and be dressed in clean clothes before leaving for school.	You must look decent before leaving for school.
You must clean your room on Saturday before going out to play. By clean, I mean all toys picked up, clothes put away or in the hamper, vacuum the floor, dust the shelves and window ledges.	You must clean your room on Saturday before going out to play. I want a complete job.

(2) The consequences for following the rule should be easily applied and known to be reinforcing.

THIS WAY	NOT THIS WAY
Eat your breakfast before the school bus comes and you won't go to school hungry.	Eat your breakfast on time or you will miss the bus. (Nick would rather miss the bus.)
When you hang up your coat and hat, you can join us for dinner.	When you hang up your coat and hat, you can set the table.

3. Guidelines for using rules[3]

a. Institute new rules one at a time.

b. When a rule is broken, ask the child to state the rule he or she broke as part of the correction.

c. When a rule is broken, have the correct behavior

---

3. Becker, Parents Are Teachers, p. 151. Used by permission.

performed before the child does anything else, if it
is possible.

    d. Use reminders to teach rules and then phase them out
(for example, signs, notes, charts, check lists).

10
min.

BREAK

III. ROLE PLAY AND PROCESS NONVERBAL COMMUNICATION

OBJECTIVES: To help parents learn to listen more effectively to
their children and each other in order to facilitate adjustment
in the family. To help parents learn to attend to nonverbal
communication and to convey acceptance to those who are speaking.

10
min.

Effective listening consists of several skills: using nonverbal
communication to show attentiveness and interest, identifying feelings, and paraphrasing or reflecting. In this section, participants
are introduced to nonverbal communication.

A. Exercise

"It is really impossible not to communicate. In a relationship
we are always communicating, even with silence. Many messages
are sent nonverbally. I would like one of you (participant or
co-leader) to talk to me for a few minutes about any topic which
interests you and I will listen to you."

1. Arrange two chairs facing each other where all participants
can observe the interaction between you and the speaker.
2. Make numerous nonverbal mistakes in listening. Mistakes might
include:

    Poor eye contact

Poor body posture, for example, not facing the speaker
or slouching

Facial expression that conveys lack of acceptance,
frowns or scowls

Groans that convey a lack of acceptance.

3. Ask the group members to identify the listening mistakes you
made.

4. Emphasize the importance of nonverbal communication when
listening and give these guidelines:

Establish good eye contact and maintain it.

Face the speaker and lean forward a little.

Facial expressions should convey interest and acceptance
of the speaker, not necessarily agreement with the
speaker.

Occasional vertical nodding of the head and short
expressions like "uh-huh," or "I see" help.

10
min.

B. List on a chalkboard or flipchart these five rules to follow
in order to listen effectively:[4]

1. Put your own feelings and thoughts aside and put yourself in
the other person's shoes.

2. Listen to the words. Watch for such nonverbal clues as voice
level, eyes, hands, and posture.

3. Listen for feelings and try to determine what is really going
on inside the person who is speaking.

4. Show your acceptance and desire to understand through good eye
contact, posture, and gestures.

5. Acceptance is not to be confused with agreement. You can

---

4. Bernard Guerney, Relationship Enhancement (San Francisco: Jossey-
Bass, 1977). Adapted with permission.

56

disagree with a person's perception or opinion and still accept him or her. However, you cannot disagree with a person's feelings although you may have different feelings.

20 min.
C. Ask the participants to form nonspouse pairs to practice the above nonverbal behaviors associated with effective listening. Observe each pair practicing and assist as needed. It is important for you to help structure the interaction while maintaining a very supportive and encouraging relationship with the participants.

"In order to learn any skill it is important to practice. We have identified some of the adjustment issues faced by children in stepfamilies and have looked at ways to improve listening skills. One of the most important things we can do for our children is to really listen to them. I would like for you to pair off with another person, someone other than your spouse, and practice the nonverbal behavior associated with effective listening. The person who plays the role of speaker should choose a subject to talk about that he or she has some strong feelings concerning. For example, the speaker could talk about something wonderful that happened recently or something frustrating or disappointing. Move your chairs so you are facing one another. Decide who will be the listener and who will speak. I will move around the room and listen in on your conversations and provide suggestions and guidance."

10 min
IV. HOMEWORK

A. "Become more aware of other people's listening skills this week. This can be done whenever you interact with others--at

work, at home, in the supermarket--or when you have the opportunity to observe other people talking with one another. Notice
what people do that makes you think they are listening to you or
that makes you think they are not listening."

B. "Become more aware of your children's feelings this week by
using the guidelines you practiced this evening. Make a point
of listening to one or more of your children for at least five
minutes during the week."

C. Have participants turn to the "List of Feelings" (numbered 2C)
in their workbooks and briefly discuss it. The purpose of this
list is to help participants become more aware of the great
variety of feelings their children may express. Tell them they
will use this page again next week.

D. Ask each couple to:
1. Identify a behavior in one of their children that they want
    to change. Set up a natural or logical consequence for the
    behavior and give it a try during the next week.
2. Talk with their children about a family rule they would like
    to establish, following the guidelines.

V. EVALUATION OF SESSION 2

Have each participant complete the evaluation form for Session 2,
numbered 2D.

Suggestions for Groups with Different Needs and Backgrounds
Attempting to convince a parent to give up physical punishment may
alienate some parents. If one of your group members insists that

children should obey and that spanking is a parent's right, it is best
to paraphrase what the parent has said in order to let the person know
you have heard them. After paraphrasing their feelings you can present
the use of natural and logical consequences as another way to approach
some of the problems. In other words, present natural and logical
consequences as an alternative way that parents may want to try. Be
aware that different ethnic and socio-economic groups may have different expectations and goals for their children.

Have participants identify some of their goals. For example, you might
say: "We know that most parents want their children to be happy and
honest because they value happiness and honesty. Each of us has a
somewhat different set of goals for our children. For example, I
would like my child to be (name one of your goals). I'd like to know
what some of your goals are for your children." In lower-income
families, obedience is frequently mentioned as a major goal. If this
appears to be a goal for the majority of your group, allow time for
discussion. Parents need to be heard and believe that their goals
are respected. There may be some conflict between the means to achieve
goals at this point, that is, physical punishment versus natural and
logical consequences.

Homework (IV)
Set up the expectation that everyone will do the activities at home
and that everyone will be contributing an experience they have had in
the next session. You might say: "By doing some of the activities
we have been doing during class at home, you will have the chance to
see which of the exercises fit your family situation and help you
with discipline. This week I would like each of you to make a point
to listen to one or more of your children for at least five minutes
and secondly, identify a behavior in one of your children you want to

change. Then discuss with your partner and your child a natural or logical consequence for that behavior. Try just one out this week and see how it works. Don't forget to follow the guidelines. Next week we'll share our experiences. In this way, we'll learn from each other."

Session 2 Worksheet

2A—Guidelines for Using Consequences*

1. Provide choices.

    Examples of choices phrased in a respectful manner:
    "Michelle, we're trying to watch television. You may settle down
    and watch the program with us or leave the room. You decide
    which you'd rather do." Or, "If you plan to go outside after
    school, you'll need to change your clothes." The choice is
    obvious. To state the alternate choice would be unnecessary.
    Some logical consequences involve stating your intentions and
    letting the child decide how to respond. "I'm willing to wash
    only the clothes that are in the hamper."

2. As you follow through with a consequence, give assurance that
    there will be an opportunity to change the decision later.
    a. Mother (following through matter-of-factly): "I see you have
        decided to leave the room. Feel free to come back when you
        are ready to settle down."
    b. Father (following through matter-of-factly): "I see you
        haven't changed your clothes as requested, so I assume you
        have decided to stay in today and try again tomorrow."

3. If the misbehavior is repeated, extend the time that must elapse
    before the child may try again.
    "I see that you're still not ready to settle down and have decided
    to leave the room. You may try again tomorrow night."
    "Because you went outside again without changing your clothes

---

*"Adapted from Systematic Training for Effective Parenting (STEP):
Parent's Handbook. Copyright 1976, by Don Dinkmeyer and Gary McKay.
Published by American Guidance Service, Publishers' Building, Circle
Pines, MN 55014."

first, you will have to stay in for the next two days. Then you can try again."

4. To make sure your action is not punishment, but an expression of logical consequences:
    Show an "open" attitude; give the child a choice and accept the child's decision.
    Use a friendly tone of voice which expresses good will.
    Make sure the consequence is logically related to the misbehavior.

2B—Guidelines for Making Rules[*]

1. Where possible, rules should be short, stated positively, and easy to remember.

THIS WAY	NOT THIS WAY
Homework before television.	If you don't get your homework done, you can't watch television.
Wash hands before eating.	You can't eat unless you wash your hands.

2. Rules should specify a behavior and a consequence.

THIS WAY	NOT THIS WAY
You make your bed before breakfast.	Make your bed each morning.
Dishes must be washed before you can watch television.	Dishes must be washed each night.
Clean your room on Saturday before going out to play.	Clean your room each Saturday.

3. Rules should be stated so that they can be easily enforced.

a. It should be easy to know whether the rule was followed or not.

THIS WAY	NOT THIS WAY
You must wash your hands and face, comb your hair and be dressed in clean clothes before leaving for school.	You must look decent before leaving for school.
You must clean your room on Saturday before going out to play. By clean, I mean all toys picked up, clothes put in the hamper, vacuum the floor, dust the shelves and window ledges.	You must clean your room on Saturday before going out to play. I want a complete job.

---

[*]Wesley Becker, _Parents Are Teachers_ (Champaign, Ill.: Research Press, 1971), pp. 148-151. Used by permission.

b. The consequences for following the rule should be easily applied
    and known to be reinforcing.

THIS WAY	NOT THIS WAY
Eat your breakfast before the	Eat your breakfast on time or
school bus comes and you	you will miss the bus. (Nick
won't go to school hungry.	would rather miss the bus.)
When you hang up your coat	When you hang up your coat and
and hat, you can join us	hat, you can set the table.
for dinner.	

c. The consequences for not following the rule should be easily
    applied and known to be effective.

d. Be sure the rule is one you can teach to your child.

Guidelines for Using Rules
1. Institute new rules one at a time.
2. When a rule is broken, ask the child to state the rule he or she
    broke as part of the correction.
3. When a rule is broken, have the correct behavior performed before
    the child does anything else, if it is possible.
4. Use reminders to teach rules and then phase them out, for
    example, signs, notes, charts, and check lists.
5. Ignore protests about rules.

2C--LIST OF FEELINGS

Mad, tender, failing, agonized, horrified, fearful, hurt, inadequate, masculine, feminine, used, bumbling, insensitive, annoyed, guilty, rejected, lonely, alone, sad, melancholy, dumb, natural, shrinking, lacking, insufficient, who cares, morbid, unwholesome, definite, brave, ashamed, irritable, terrible, miserable, serene, panicked, punished, dissolute, wistful, selfish, moping, mournful, happy, comforted, positive, negative, jealous, unique, eerie, complete, incomplete, like a ping-pong game, embarrassed, dignified, undignified, loathing, helpless, useless, reassured, magnanimous, forgotten, expectant, dull, icky, delighted, disappointed, touched, cowardly, burdensome, burdened, squeamish, moved, up tight, affectionate, foolish, intimate, dominated, defensive, furious, excited, crushed, stupid, artificial, satisfied, bubbly, nervous, self-sufficient, strong, weak, compatible, incompatible, close, trusting, confident, consoled, apprehensive, degraded, responsive, confused, trusted, cheated, trapped, bewildered, aghast, mean, aware, hypocritical, cut-off, out on a limb, courageous, tearful, relieved, daring, patronizing, clean, tense, betrayed, pained, bugged, wounded, protective, vulnerable, exposed, dissatisfied, immature, leery, emotionally drained, doubtful, misgiving, changed, dread, monotony, anticipation, excitement, cozy, upset, gay, charmed, charming, self pity, beautiful, growing, lousy, poor, blah, misunderstood, cold, calculating, craving, empty, strange, disloyal, loyal, inhuman, crazy, unsound, unfinished, incompetent, petrified, nauseated, unreal, phony, false, sickened, repulsed, condescending.

Session 2 Worksheet

2D--EVALUATION OF SESSION 2

Please rate the following items according to how helpful you think
they are/will be to you in your stepfamily situation.

1 = Very helpful

2 = Helpful

3 = Unhelpful

4 = Very unhelpful

_____1. Discussion of the homework assignment from last week.

_____2. Discussion regarding role expectations.

_____3. Discussion of natural and logical consequences.

_____4. Discussion of family rules.

_____5. Discussion of nonverbal communication.

_____6. Discussion of listening guidelines.

_____7. Practice of listening to another person.

What was _most_ helpful in this session?

What was _least_ helpful in this session?

How could this session have been more helpful to you?

SESSION 3

I. DISCUSS HOMEWORK

OBJECTIVES: To encourage homework completion by asking for feedback and questions.

10
min.

A. Ask the participants what they observed and experienced as they watched other people's listening skills during the past week.

B. Ask the participants for feedback regarding their experiences listening to their children. Be aware that their skill level at this point may be low.

C. Ask the participants if they had any problems establishing consequences or rules last week.

II. ADJUSTMENT ISSUES FACED BY CHILDREN IN STEPFAMILIES

OBJECTIVES: To help parents gain an understanding of the typical adjustment problems for children in stepfamilies.

Present all of Part II following a lecture and discussion format. It is vital that you show the participants how each session is a continuation of the previous session.

"In the first session we looked at some of the adjustment issues faced by children in stepfamilies. Tonight we're going to look at a few more adjustment issues and emphasize the importance of good listening in helping children. Children in stepfamilies can and do make the necessary adjustments and you can play an important role in helping them make these adjustments."

20
min.

A. <u>Dealing With Loss</u>

Present the following to stimulate discussion.

1. "Most children in stepfamilies have experienced a sense of loss, either as a result of one of their parents dying or as a result of a divorce. Adults experience this sense of loss as well, although in the case of divorce they usually adjusted to the loss before the children do. A five-stage loss model helps us understand how adults and children adjust to loss:

"<u>Denial</u>. The first reaction to divorce is often denial. Denial helps a person deal with the shock associated with the loss. It typically occurs immediately after learning about the loss, but can continue for a long time and thus inhibit adjustment to the loss.

"<u>Guilt</u>. A person may blame himself or herself for the loss and spend a great deal of energy thinking about what he or she did that caused the loss or what could have been done to prevent it from occuring.

"<u>Anger</u>. Anger is a natural reaction to loss. It may arise from feeling abandoned or from the frustration of not being able to change the situation. Regardless of the cause of the anger, it is only the tip of an 'emotional iceberg'. Beneath anger there are usually feelings of hurt, fear, and rejection. The following diagram illustrates this point." (Prepare a

flipchart sketch or hand out copies of the illustration prior
to the workshop session.)

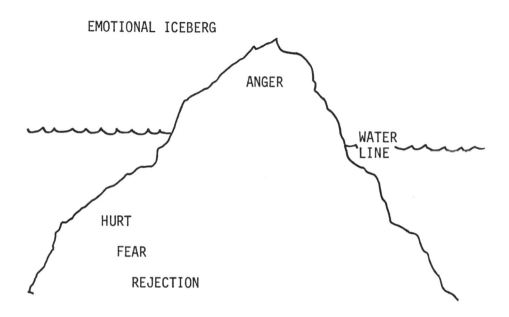

EMOTIONAL ICEBERG

ANGER

WATER
LINE

HURT

FEAR

REJECTION

"Grief. Experiencing and expressing grief regarding a loss
is a vital part of adjusting to the loss.

"Acceptance is the final stage. People typically experience
denial, guilt, anger, and grief before reaching a point of
acceptance."

2. Ask participants for questions and personal examples of
this five-stage phenomenon.

3. "Remarriage affects a child's adjustment to the previous
loss of a parent. Some children may not experience a sense of
loss until the time of remarriage. In the divorce-remarriage

process a parent may seek emotional support from his or her children and this added closeness to one parent often helps compensate for the separation from the other parent. However, when the parent with whom the children are living remarries, the children may think they have now lost this parent as well, and their sense of loss becomes acute.

"If remarriage occurs a short time after death or divorce, mourning and grieving may not be over yet for the children, and, as a result, they may not be prepared to accept a new adult into their lives. If the new partner is presented to the children as a replacement for the lost parent, resentment and grief may become apparent. The children may see the parent's remarriage as a betrayal of the former spouse.

"If remarriage takes place after a longer period of time, the special bond between parent and children may be threatened and resentment and grief often occur. In some cases, children are not included in the courtship and feel abandoned while their parent is feeling euphoric. Children may think that their parent's personality has changed. For example, one teenager said to her father, 'Your personality as I knew it was gone, and the man I knew as you was completely submerged into your relationship with Christy (his new wife). There was no way of knowing you as an individual person anymore, so essentially you were completely gone. No longer did I feel as though I had a father at all because I didn't know you anymore'."[1]

---

1. Visher and Visher, Stepfamilies, p. 165.

<table>
<tr><td>10
min.</td><td>4. Ask participants to determine where their children are in the loss adjustment process and then share that information with a person near them, someone other than their spouse. Participants should form pairs and move their chairs close together for discussion.</td></tr>
</table>

"I would like you to relate this information to your own children. Try to identify where one or more of your children are in their adjustment process. You may identify some be-haviors or feelings of your children which give you information about their adjustment. Then turn to someone other than your spouse and share that information."

<table>
<tr><td>10
min.</td><td>B.</td><td>Fantasizing a Reunion of Parents</td></tr>
</table>

1. "Even after the remarriage of both parents, children often cling to the fantasy that their natural parents will be re-united. Any friendly interchange between the natural parents may be used by the children to convince themselves that the fantasy is true. They may repeatedly ask the same basic questions, 'Aren't you and Dad (Mom) getting back together?'

"The children may consciously or unconsciously attempt to split up the new couple as the first step in making their fantasy come true."

2. After presenting this information about the fantasy of reunion, ask the participants if they have seen this fantasy expressed by their own children. Briefly discuss their experiences.

10
min.

C. <u>What Parents Can Do to Facilitate the Adjustment of Their</u>
<u>Children as They Deal With Loss and Fantasize about Their</u>
<u>Natural Parents Reuniting</u>

1. "In terms of adjusting to loss, parents need to allow
their children to acknowledge their feelings. Telling
children they shouldn't feel angry, for example, makes it
very difficult for them to deal with the anger and work
through it. Telling children to 'be brave' and that 'big boys
and girls don't cry' squelches their natural expression of
grief. Basically then, parents can help their children adjust
to loss by helping them identify their feelings, accepting
them, and allowing them to express their feelings freely.

"In terms of helping children deal with the fantasy of their
natural parents reuniting, parents need to listen for the
feelings behind the fantasies and be willing to patiently
deal with the same questions again and again. Questions
like: 'Mom, do you think that Dad still cares for you?'"

These suggestions emphasize the importance of stepparents
becoming skilled listeners.

2. Ask the participants for additional ways to handle fantasy
reuniting problems based on their own experiences.

10
min.

BREAK

III. EFFECTIVE LISTENING--SKILLS BUILDING

OBJECTIVES: To help parents become more aware of feelings. To help parents recognize appropriate conditions for using effective listening. Practice effective listening.

Point out the continuity between the nonverbal listening skills taught in Session 2 with listening for feelings and paraphrasing taught in this session.

"Last week we looked at the importance of nonverbal communication-- such things as eye contact, body posture, facial expression, and nodding of the head. Tonight we are going to learn more about how to be an effective listener. We will begin by discussing typical mistakes we make when listening to children and then look at the guidelines for effective listening."

10
min.

A. Role Play and Process Ineffective Listening
   1. Role Play
   Ask your coleader or a group participant to play the role of a fifteen-year-old son or daughter who storms into the house and announces: "I hate school. It's a bore. This school isn't half as nice as _my_ school. The kids here are dumb and they hate me. I don't care if I flunk out." The person playing the role of the adolescent can take this basic script and develop it however he or she likes. As "parent" you respond to the fifteen-year-old in judgmental and unaccepting ways. Typical responses you might make are:
      Ordering or giving directions: "You get in there and do your homework."
      Moralizing: "You shouldn't hate anyone or anything."

<u>Advising</u>: "Why don't you invite kids over and get acquainted?"

<u>Using logic</u>: "You're just not used to your new school."

<u>Judging or blaming</u>: "If you will just try a little harder."

<u>Reassuring or sympathizing</u>: "It will get better."

2. After the brief role play, provide the participants with a list of the six typical responses listed above (for example, ordering and giving directions), and ask them to identify the statements made by the facilitator that fit each category.

3. Discuss why these responses are barriers to communication. Suggested reasons are as follows:[2]

They communicate a desire to <u>change</u> the child rather than a desire to accept him or her.

They take responsibility for solving the problem away from the child and imply an assumption that he or she is unable to handle the situation.

They create resistance and defensiveness.

They carry hidden messages such as:

"I don't accept you."

"I don't trust you."

"Your feelings are not valid."

"You're wrong, bad, etc."

"I don't really care how you feel."

"You are misperceiving reality."

They often cause the child to stop talking.

---

2. From <u>P.E.T.: Parent Effectiveness Training Instructor Guide</u>. Copyright 1977, by Thomas Gordon.

4. Review the five rules for effective listening. Use an overhead projector or put them on a chalkboard or flipchart.

a. Put your own feelings and thoughts aside and put yourself in the other person's shoes.

b. Listen to words. Watch for nonverbal clues: voice level, eyes, hands, posture. Listen for feelings and try to determine what is really going on inside the person who is speaking.

c. Show your acceptance and desire to understand through good eye contact, posture, and gestures.

d. Acceptance is not to be confused with agreement. You can disagree with a person's perception or opinion and still accept him or her. You cannot disagree with their feelings although you may have different feelings.

e. Actions need to be consistent with words. If they are not consistent, the listener loses his or her credibility.

5. Insure participants that learning to be a better listener is not as complicated as it may sound. Tell them to keep the guidelines for effective listening handy as they practice. Ask for questions. Stress that tonight the focus is on the other two skills that are part of effective listening: Listening for feelings and paraphrasing.

B. Focus on Feelings
Present this section using a lecture and discussion format.

"Definition of feelings. Feelings are spontaneous reactions to our thoughts and expectations. For example, 'When I think you intentionally ignore me I feel rejected'. Or, 'I expected you to meet me for lunch at noon but you arrived at 12:30 and so I felt angry'.

"Identification of feelings. Although feelings occur inside your body, there are usually outward indications of your feelings. For example, tensed muscles and flushed skin may be outward signs of anger. Tears may indicate sadness. Laughing and smiling may reflect happiness. Identify a feeling indicated by the following physical signs." (Refer them to the handout on feelings they received last week, 2C.) "For example,

Physical Sign	Feeling
Sweating	Nervous
Avoiding eye contact	Ashamed, embarrassed
Getting quiet	Angry, intimidated
Laughing	Happy, elated
Rapid heartbeat	Fearful

"Dealing with feelings. It is impossible to control feelings by ignoring them or denying them. It is futile and harmful for a parent to insist that children feel certain ways or that they justify, explain, or apologize for their feelings. Consequently, it is vital for parents to identify their children's feelings and accept these feelings even though they may wish that the children felt differently. This helps children have greater control over their feelings rather than being controlled by them."

"Mixed feelings. It's common for all people to experience mixed feelings. For example, a person might feel angry, sad, and confused at the same time and thus have difficulty understanding what he or she feels. Or, the feelings might be in conflict. For example, a child might feel secure with his or her stepfather but also feel disloyal to his or her biological father. Parents can help their children sort out their feelings by using a listening skill called 'paraphrasing'."

<table>
<tr><td>10
min.</td><td>C. <u>Paraphrasing</u></td></tr>
</table>

C. <u>Paraphrasing</u>

   1. Role play.

   To introduce paraphrasing, ask your co-leader or a group member to engage in a role play with you. Arrange two chairs facing one another in a place visible to the entire group.

   2. Model paraphrasing.

   Ask the group what they observed, identifying the various components of the skill.

   3. Define paraphrasing.

   "Paraphrasing involves identifying the main thoughts and feelings being expressed by a speaker and stating them back to the speaker in your own words. For example, a child might say, 'I hate that class, there is no way I can pass it'. The parent might paraphrase by saying, 'You're feeling pretty discouraged about that class'."

   4. Rules for paraphrasing.

   "Don't interpret what the person is saying by adding your own explanation or reason for what they are experiencing. For example, your son might say, 'I don't want to go visit my Dad this week'. A parent might say, 'That's what you said last time and after you went you were glad you did. I think you'll be glad you went this time also'. Such a response ignores what your son is really feeling and discourages him from talking more about it.

77

"Don't make suggestions about how the person can solve his or her discomfort. This also fails to acknowledge the speaker's feelings and implies that the person is unable to handle his or her own affairs and thus needs some expert advice from you.

"Don't judge what the speaker has said. Remember that the speaker is risking being open with you. If a person concludes that you think he or she is wrong to think and feel a certain way, communication will stop."

5
min.

5. Practice identifying feelings and paraphrasing.
Read statements on Worksheet 3A and ask the participants to identify the child's feelings and suggest possible responses.

6. When paraphrasing is appropriate.
"In terms of the speaker, paraphrasing is appropriate only when a person is experiencing a problem. A child's problem may be apparent through verbal or nonverbal expressions (for example, 'I'm worried', or 'Mommy, did you ever worry about your Mommy and Daddy dying?') or crying or sulking. If troublesome feelings or problems are not present in a person, the person will likely think paraphrasing is a crazy game. For example, a child says, 'Mom, I would like to go over to Bill's and play basketball', and Mom responds, 'Oh, you want to go over to Bill's to play basketball'. Paraphrasing on such occasions is inappropriate.

"In terms of the parent or listener, he or she must: feel accepting of the child or other person; want to help, not simply 'turn on a technique'; be willing to take enough time to listen; and trust that the speaker will be able to solve his or her own problem."

15
min.

    D. Practicing Effective Listening

Have the participants form a pair with someone other than their spouse to practice effective listening. Stress that they should first identify feelings and then paraphrase. Each person in the pair should assume the role of speaker and then the listener. The speaker should identify one of the adjustment issues experienced by one of his or her children and role play that child's typical ways of talking about the issue. The listener should use appropriate effective listening skills. Circulate among the pairs, reinforcing appropriate skills and offering suggestions for skill improvement when necessary.

IV. HOMEWORK

Ask the group members to:

A. Complete the written workbook exercise, "Identifying Feelings and Paraphrasing" (numbered 3B) and bring it with them to the next session.

B. Practice using effective listening for two ten-minute periods with one of their children. They are to identify as many of the children's feelings as they can and practice paraphrasing as is appropriate for the occasion.

C. Read the following in their workbooks: "3C--Developmental Stages and Reactions to Divorce" and "3D--When does a Child Need a Professional Counselor?" and relate them to their own children.

D. Read "3E--The Benefits of Effective Listening."

V. EVALUATION OF SESSION 3

Have each participant complete the evaluation form for Session 3, see
Worksheet 3F.

Suggestions for Groups with Different Needs and Backgrounds
Session 3 is the first session with a specific written homework assignment. By this time you should be able to determine if your group is
working with the ideas presented at home and if they are likely to
follow through on an assignment. You may decide that one of the
assignments is sufficient. If you decide to assign the written exercise, be sure to do three or four of the statements as a group. When
you assign it, point out that this is the same exercise as the role
play and that they may want to role play the rest of the statements
with their partner.

3A--Role Play for Session 3

Instructions: The group leader plays the role of a child. Ask one participant to identify the child's feelings and the person sitting next to him or her to provide an effective listening response.

CHILD'S FEELING	CHILD'S ROLE STATEMENT
Discouraged Disappointed	"Boy, my new dad sure is dumb. He doesn't even know how to play Star Wars!"
Excited Happy	"Oh boy, only ten more days until I get to go to my real Dad's house!!"
Worried Lonely	"Mommy, when is my <u>real</u> Dad coming back?"
Bored Stumped	"Gee, I'm not having any fun. I can't think of anything to do."
Deflated	"My new Mom gives me too much housework to do. I can never get it all done. What will I do?"
Left Behind Lonely	"All the other kids went to the beach. I don't have <u>anyone</u> to play with."
Resentful	"I want to wear my hair long.-- It's <u>my hair</u> isn't it?"
Guilty	"Dad, I'm sorry that Jamie and I used to argue so much when you and Mom were married."

3B--Identifying Feelings and Paraphrasing

Read each statement, identify the feelings of the child, and write an effective listening response you would make.

Feelings	Statement	Paraphrase
	1. "My <u>real</u> Dad always caught fish when he took me fishing."	
	2. "Why don't you get off my case. You're always after me."	
	3. "I'm not going back to school. Everybody looks at me like I'm some kind of weirdo."	
	4. "Do you think my Dad will come to my recital?"	
	5. "I don't have to obey you, you're not my <u>real</u> Dad."	
	6. "Dad, when are you and Mom getting back together?"	
	7. "Will I still be able to go visit Grandma?"	
	8. "I'm not going to share my room with those guys. They tear up everything I have."	
	9. "I'm trying to like Bill (new stepfather), but he can't do anything like Dad does."	

Feelings	Statement	Paraphrase
	10. "This pizza isn't nearly as good as <u>my</u> Mom makes (addressed to a new step-mother)."	

3C—Developmental Stages and Reactions to Divorce*

Preschool children

Very young children (18-24 months) have little differentiation from parents and if close contact with a careparent is maintained, infants experience little disruption.

Incomplete mourning of loss is a basic problem for children in re-married families. They go through the mourning process more slowly than adults.

After a divorce young children may become very needy in terms of atten-tion and affection, some regression may occur. Divorce and remarriage are often confused and both are associated with loss.

Preschool children need the opportunity to express feelings and to have a sustained relationship with a supportive parent or stepparent.

Children 6-12 years

These children are beginning to differentiate themselves from their parents and express their feelings relatively easily.

A sense of guilt at causing the disintegration of the parents' mar-riage frequently remains. Often fantasy is common. It is important to build this age child's self-esteem and reassure him or her that the divorce did not occur due to the child being bad or unlovable.

This age boy often identifies strongly with his father and often worries about his father and retains a fierce loyalty to him.

One concern of this age child is what to tell their friends about their family. They may feel uncomfortable being labelled a "step-child."

Reminding these children of the great number of stepchildren in the world and building self-esteem is important here.

---

*Visher and Visher, Stepfamilies.

Adolescent stepchildren

They tend to deal with loss by withdrawing from both of their parents and by taking an "I don't care" attitude. They do care and need help working through their feelings.

Adolescents have differentiated themselves from their parents and so may be expected to be away from their parents more than a younger child.

Teenage daughters identify strongly with their natural mothers and often resent women who replace their mothers. Teenage daughters also show a good deal of competitiveness with stepmothers for the fathers' attention. Teenage boys may feel angry that their fathers have been betrayed by their mothers. They feel confused and unable to identify with stepfathers who are unlike their natural fathers.

Adolescence is a time when a child who has been living with the mother often wishes to go live with the father. This is often a healthy move for the teenage boy because he can identify with a male model. Teenage girls who ask to live with their fathers are often desirous of wanting to "win" their fathers away from any female rivals. This can be a dangerous move for a female adolescent.

Remarried adults need to be sensitive to the need of adolescent children to be independent. Stepparents should not try to become the "parent" but rather a good friend. Clashes with teenagers are common in intact families, and in stepfamilies the frequency and intensity often become unbearable.

3D—When Does a Child Need a Professional Counselor?*

The child who needs therapy is generally one who has exhibited difficulties for a significant period of time prior to the separation and whose symptoms have intensified as a result of the separation.

A key principle is the <u>duration</u> of the difficulties. Problems to look for are:

A deterioration of academic performance and classroom behavior

Intense sibling fighting is a poor criterion to use. Instead, examine the child's peer relationships. A child with significant difficulties in peer relationships usually needs therapy.

When refusal to cooperate at home is so marked that the child does practically nothing around the house and when frequent power struggles appear to be the rule, the child may need treatment.

---

*Excerpted from <u>The Parents' Book Above Divorce</u> by Richard A. Gardner. Copyright c 1977 by Richard A. Gardner, M.D. Reprinted by permission of Doubleday & Company, Inc.

3E--BENEFITS OF EFFECTIVE LISTENING*

1. It shows the person that you are interested in him or her.
2. It proves that not only have you heard, you understood.
3. It is your check on the accuracy of your decoding of the other's message.
4. It gives the speaker a chance to ventilate, to feel relieved, to release. Feelings can be transitory.
5. Effective listening communicates acceptance of the person.
6. It fosters the speaker doing his or her own defining of the problem and problem solving.
7. It fosters the person moving from superficial to deeper, more basic problems.
8. It frequently fosters insights--new ways of seeing things, new attitudes, new behaviors, new understanding of self.
9. It promotes a more intimate and warm relationship. The speaker feels more warm and loving toward you. You better understand the speaker and feel more loving toward him or her.
10. It helps a person grow toward being an internal problem solver, toward being less dependent on others for solutions, toward being more self-responsible, more self-directing--a master of his or her own fate or destiny.

---

*From: <u>P.E.T.: Parent Effectiveness Training Instructor Guide</u>.
Copyright 1970, by Thomas Gordon.

3F--Evaluation of Session Three

Please rate the following items according to how helpful you think they are or will be to you in your stepfamily situation:

1 = Very helpful

2 = Helpful

3 = Unhelpful

4 = Very unhelpful

____1.   Discussion of last week's homework.

____2.   Discussion of how children deal with loss as a result of divorce or death.

____3.   Discussion of how remarriage affects a child's adjustment.

____4.   Discussion of how children often fantasize a reunion of their parents.

____5.   Discussion of communication barriers.

____6.   Learning to identify feelings and paraphrase.

____7.   Practice of effective listening.

What was <u>most</u> helpful in this session?

What was <u>least</u> helpful in this session?

How could this session have been more helpful to you?

SESSION 4

I. DISCUSS HOMEWORK

OBJECTIVES: To encourage participants to complete homework by
asking for feedback and questions. To provide clarification
regarding any information provided in Session 3.

10
min.

A. Ask the participants for feedback regarding the readings on
developmental stages, when children need a therapist, and the
benefits of effective listening.

B. Ask for comments regarding the homework exercise in identifying feelings and paraphrasing.

C. Ask for feedback on their listening practice exercise with
their children.

II. ADJUSTMENT ISSUES FACED BY PARENTS IN STEPFAMILIES

OBJECTIVES: To establish group closeness and allow for catharsis
on common issues and problems for stepparents. To provide
insight on adjustment issues faced by parents in stepfamilies,
and to suggest ways for these issues to be resolved.

"In Session 1 we began looking at some of the issues faced by parents
in stepfamilies. We looked at the confusion that often exists regarding the roles stepparents are expected to play in stepfamilies.
We discussed the importance of discipline in a family, how it is
crucial in uniting a stepfamily and how the use of consequences and
family rules can help parents discipline their children. In this

89

session we shall look at some additional adult issues: concerns regarding finances, ex-spouses, and visitation. We shall also discuss the importance of the husband-wife relationship. We shall look first at financial concerns."

10 min.

A. <u>Financial Concerns</u>

Present the following to stimulate discussion.

"In regard to receiving child support payments, a common complaint made by wives is that their ex-husbands are not sending them the money they owe them. The percentage of husbands who live up to their support commitments over several years is very small. At present, the courts are doing very little to enforce payments. It is wise to make reasonable efforts to get the payments; but if a woman's efforts fail, she should consider other alternatives. It is important to remember that the emotional drain on herself and her children resulting from maintaining hostilities toward an ex-husband cannot be counted in dollars.

"Children should be allowed to have a good relationship with their father in spite of his failure to pay child support. On the other hand, a father who fails to make payments should not be protected by the mother. Children need an accurate picture of their parents. It is also not wise to use visitation as a weapon to get more money or in some way demand more from an ex-husband. This only hurts the children."

"In regard to sending child-support payments, the money should be sent to the mother, not the child, unless the child is an adult. Sending the money to the child can perpetuate conflict between the ex-spouses involved. The children need to be made aware of the source of the money they receive.

90

"Couples in stepfamilies frequently experience financial difficulties as they try to make ends meet. There are often child-
support payments going out and others coming in. This can
create conflicts as decisions are made regarding who will handle
which funds and how the family finances will be apportioned to
various existing needs. It is important for couples to reach
an agreement on handling money. Honest communication and problem
solving skills can help."

Ask for questions, comments, and suggestions on financial issues.

20 min.

B. Ex-Spouses and Visitation Concerns
    Present the following to stimulate discussion.
        1. "Children are sometimes used as pawns in struggles between
        their natural parents. For example, a father purposely shows
        up late to pick up the children for a visit with him. Or a
        mother has a nonchalant attitude about getting the children
        ready for the visit. Or a mother doesn't let the father have
        the children because he's late with a support payment. This
        punishes the children for the action of their father."

        2. "Ex-spouses may engage in 'pain games' that damage their
        relationship further and hurt their relationships with their
        children. Such games identified by The Menninger Foundation's
        Community Service Office include:[1]
            "Disneyland Daddy: In this game, the father takes the
            children to expensive, fun places to show them how great a
            dad he is and how boring the children's mother is. This

_____

1. "Pain games" are copyrighted by Community Service Office, The
Menninger Foundation, 1983. Use by permission.

91

may cause resentment in the mother, and it is expensive
and stressful for the father. Eventually the children
see through the game.

"I Spy: The children are used as pawns to spy on the
activities of the ex-spouse. Comments such as the following might be made: 'Who is your father dating now?
Her? How could he? Are they living together?' This
situation harms the relationship between parents and
children and breeds bad feelings between ex-spouses.

"Messenger: In this pain game, the child serves as a
messenger between the two ex-spouses. Statements such
as the following might be made: 'Tell your father that
the roof leaks. And, he needs to come over and fix your
bike. Also, ask him why his child support check is late.
Again, this harms relationships and breeds resentment.

"I Wish: Initially, 'I Wish' is not a game but a normal
postdivorce response, expressing a willingness or desire
for a marital reconciliation, the hesitation to accept
the finality of the guilt and discomfort associated
with the decision. 'I Wish' becomes a game when
parents don't give their children a clear message that
the divorce is final."

3. "Problems frequently arise immediately after children
return home after visiting the noncustodial parent, usually
the father. The restlessness of the children is interpreted
differently by the father and mother. The father concludes
that he is the best parent because the children are unhappy
to be back with their ogre mother. The mother sees the
children's restlessness as resulting from tensions created by
the father or indignities they have suffered at his hands.

It is important to remember that ex-spouses have a tendency to exaggerate the detrimental effects of one another's behavior on the children."

4. "Non-custodial parents, usually fathers, frequently experience a loss of self-esteem about not being able to provide their children with what they believe they should be giving them. The following suggestions may help rebuild self-esteem:

"Spend as much time with the children as is reasonably possible.

"Involve yourself in a second family.

"Find other esteem-enhancing activities--volunteer work, job, hobbies, work with religious groups."

5. Solicit questions, comments, and suggestions from the group.

5
min.

C. The Husband-Wife Relationship

1. "Parents in stepfamilies usually feel a very strong commitment to the needs of their children. Consequently, they may feel guilty taking time to be alone to nurture their husband-wife relationship. Many family life experts contend that the strength of the husband-wife relationship is a basic determinant of the success of a stepfamily. Therefore, special efforts need to be made to strengthen and nurture the couple relationship. One of the best ways to improve your parenting is to build your marriage."

2. Discuss this concept with the participants. Ask them to explain why they believe this relationship has been found.

5
min.

D. <u>Other Issues Faced by Parents in Stepfamilies</u>
Ask participants to suggest and discuss other issues that are frequently faced by parents in stepfamilies.

10
min.

BREAK

III. EFFECTIVE LISTENING--SKILLS BUILDING

OBJECTIVES: To encourage spouses to begin identifying and communicating about problems and strengths in their own marriage and family relationships. To provide an opportunity for practice of effective listening.

50
min.

A. This is an opportunity for each participant to sharpen his or her listening skills. Begin this section by reviewing the guidelines for effective listening; review guidelines on nonverbal communication, listening for feelings, and paraphrasing, pages 75-78.

"During the past four weeks you have begun learning how to be a better listener. We have stressed the importance of being effective listeners with our children. However, these listening skills should also be used regularly with our partners. By being better listeners we can enrich and strengthen our marriages. For the rest of this session, I want you to practice the listening skills we have learned with your spouse. Arrange your chairs so that you have some privacy and decide which of the following issues

94

you and your spouse will talk about: finances, ex-spouses, visitation issues, or the nurturance of the husband-wife relationship."

B. Have each couple discuss the topic they selected. One spouse assumes the role of speaker while the other spouse practices effective listening. After fifteen minutes have them switch roles. Move around the room assisting the listeners. Reinforce effective listening and shape undeveloped skills.

C. After both partners have been given time to practice effective listening, re-form the larger group and have participants discuss their reactions to the exercise.

IV. HOMEWORK

10
min.

A. Discuss and assign each couple to develop a Marriage Growth Plan (see Worksheet 4A). Ask them to arrange a time and place during the next week to do the exercise. Have each couple relate their plans.

B. Encourage all participants to practice effective listening with each other and their children for at least two ten-minute periods during the next week.

C. As a group, decide on a time two months from now that you will meet again to practice the listening skills and share positive experiences. Sixty days will allow you to finish the next four sessions and still have a thirty-day follow-up meeting for those who complete all eight sessions. If this is the end of the group meetings, choose a date one month from now. Ask for a

couple to volunteer the use of their home for the follow-up
meeting. Set time, place, and other necessary arrangements.
See page 146 for details.

D. Ask for comments or questions on any aspect of the workshop.
Tell the participants who return for Sessions 5-8 that next week
they will learn effective speaking skills.

V. EVALUATION OF SESSION 4

Have participants complete the evaluation form for Session 4, numbered
4B.

4A—MARRIAGE GROWTH PLAN

The purpose of this exercise is to plan into the next month the time, resources, and energy to do something that will strengthen your marital relationship. Allow yourselves an hour to do the exercise.

A. Begin by answering the following questions:

1. What kinds of activities did we really enjoy doing together during our courtship? For example, long walks together or going to a movie.

2. What activities do married couples that I know do to enjoy themselves?

3. List ten activities that we could do together that would strengthen our marriage.

4. List ten things that <u>you could do</u> that would show your spouse that you really care about him or her.

B. Get together with your partner and share your answers to questions 1 through 3. Do not show him or her your answers to number 4 at this time.

C. Decide together on an activity that will strengthen your marriage. Make a firm plan to do the activity at least once during the next month. Be sure to answer these questions as you both plan the activity:

1. What <u>specifically</u> are we going to do?
2. On what day are we going to do it?
3. At what time are we going to do it?
4. How are we going to handle babysitting (if necessary)? Who will arrange it? When will he or she arrange it? Who should watch the children?
5. How will we get the funds to do this (if necessary)?
6. Who has responsibility for what?
7. What advance arrangements do we need to make and who will make them?

Session 4 Worksheet

4B--EVALUATION OF SESSION 4

Please rate the following items according to how helpful you think
they are/will be to you in your stepfamily situation:

1 = Very helpful

2 = Helpful

3 = Unhelpful

4 = Very unhelpful

_____1. Discussion of last week's homework.

_____2. Discussion of financial concerns.

_____3. Discussion of "pain games."

_____4. Discussion of visitation issues.

_____5. Discussion of the importance of the husband-wife relationship.

_____6. The practice of effective listening in which couples discussed
topics like finances, ex-spouses, and visitation.

What was <u>most</u> helpful in this session?

What was <u>least</u> helpful in this session?

How could this session have been more helpful to you?

SESSION 5

I. DISCUSS HOMEWORK

OBJECTIVE: To encourage homework completion by asking for feedback and questions.

10
min.

A. Ask the participants to report their feelings and questions about effective listening and the practice session they completed during the last week.

B. Ask each couple to share with the group members the marriage growth plan they constructed during the past week.

II. EFFECTIVE SPEAKING--SKILLS BUILDING

OBJECTIVES: To teach effective speaking skills that will allow self-disclosure without harming a relationship. To provide participants with an opportunity to practice effective speaking skills.

25
min.

This section focuses on learning how to self-disclose in a manner that does not hurt a relationship, for example, not using accusatory language, speaking for self, not others. Do the following role play with a member of the group. Begin by making the following statement: "You have had to tell your teenage stepson to do his chores three times. So, you are now going to confront him. 'James, when I have to keep telling you to do your chores it really irritates me. I think that you must not care about my desire to have a clean home, and that really hurts'.

"Your next statement should contain your desire--what you want the person to do specifically and behaviorally; for example, 'I want you to do your chores the first time I tell you'."

Solicit questions and comments about the role play, and then talk about the guidelines for effective speaking.

A. Guidelines for Effective Speaking
   1. "Effective listening always comes first. Being sensitive to others and letting them know that you hear them is essential before expressing your own needs or point of view. When others believe that you understand them, they will be more open to you and your opinions."

   2. "Speak for yourself, not the other person. This is done by using the pronoun 'I' rather than 'you'. Speaking for self reduces defensiveness on the part of the listener." Give an example.

   3. "Talk about specific behaviors in the other person and how they make you feel. Using the following formula can help you in developing effective speaking responses:
   'When you _____ (describe the behavior), I feel _____ (use a feeling word) because _____ (tell how the behavior affected you)'. For example: 'When you fail to clean up your room, I feel angry, because that means extra work for me'."

   4. Have the participants practice developing effective speaking responses. To do this ask them to take out a copy of the "Effective Speaking Vignettes" from their workbooks

(numbered 5A) and instruct the participants to develop responses using the formulas given above.

5. After a few minutes, ask for examples of responses to the vignettes one at a time.

25
min.
B. Gear Shifting

"When you send a message to another, that person will sometimes reply with a defensive response, such as, 'Tough!' or 'That's the last time I'll call you'. This often happens with children. When this happens, it is important that the parent be flexible and be able to shift gears back into effective listening. For example, a parent says, 'When you leave your dishes on the table I get irritated because it makes extra work for me'. In return, the child says, 'Why do I have so many chores to do?' At this point the parent should shift gears and provide an effective listening response such as, 'You think you have to do more than other people in this house and you resent that'."

1. Have the participants practice making effective speaking statements and gear-shifting. To do this, have participants form pairs. Have one pair sit together in front of the group. Give one member of the pair a card with a statement made by a parent and the other person a card with a response made by a child. The person playing the parent role reads his or her statement and the person playing the child role responds with his or her statement. The parent then shifts gears by giving an effective listening response. Coach and reinforce the pair as they practice in front of the group. The other participants should observe. Sample statements to be written on cards follow. M = for a male parent, F = for a female parent.

Gut Feeling in Parent	Parent's Statement	Child's Response
Disappointed	(M) "I'm upset when you treat your stepmother as if she doesn't belong by refusing to do what she asks you to do."	"But Dad, she's not my _real_ mom."
Disappointed	(F) "It really bothers me when you don't shoot baskets with your stepfather when he asks you to."	"Well, he doesn't play as well as my _real_ dad."
Hurt	(M) "I felt put down when you said I don't care about you when I wouldn't buy you a toy."	"My real dad buys me _everything_ I ask _him_ for."
Happy	(F) "I'm really glad that you and your stepdad had fun at the game!"	"Oh, it was okay, I guess."
Infuriated	(F) "It infuriates me when you fail to do something I ask you to do!"	"Well, I don't have to do that. I do what _my_ Dad says, not you."
Shocked	(M) "It really shocked me when you called your stepbrother that name!"	"So?"
Empathy	(F) "I understand that you can take food to your room at your mother's but around this house we eat in the kitchen."	"Boy, you sure are a crab."

2. After each pair has had an opportunity to do the exercise in front of the group, note to the participants that after they "shift gears" into listening and are sure they have shown the

other person that they understand, they can shift back into
effective speaking again.

10   BREAK
min.

III. EXERCISE--EFFECTIVE LISTENING, SPEAKING, AND GEARSHIFTING

OBJECTIVE: To provide an opportunity for practice of effective
listening, effective speaking, and gearshifting.

50   During this and the remaining sessions participants will have the
min.   opportunity to practice and sharpen their speaking and listening
skills.

A. Ask group members to complete the copy of the Family Relations
Questionnaire (FRQ) from their workbooks. It is Worksheet 5B.
Allow fifteen minutes.

B. Assign participants to form pairs with persons other than their
spouses. Pairs should determine who will be the speaker and who
will be the listener for the first practice session.

C. Instruct the speaker to choose a response from Part A of his
or her FRQ that he or she will use.
    1. If the speaker chooses a feeling response that he or she
    made, the speaker should:
        a. Describe the situation in which the response occurred
        to the listener. For example, "This happened late one
        night when I was trying to get my daughter to bed."

b. Then, make the response (role play) to the listener (as written on Part A of the FRQ). For example, "If you don't hurry up and brush your teeth, I will come in there and brush them for you!"

c. Instruct the listener to reconstruct the response so that it is an effective speaking statement and say it back to the speaker. For example, "It's really frustrating when you take so long to brush your teeth."

2. If the speaker chooses a feeling response that his or her child made, the speaker should:

a. Describe the situation in which the response occurred to the listener. For example, "This happened yesterday when I asked my stepson to do his chores."

b. Then, make the response (role play) to the listener. For example, "I don't have to mind you, you're not my real dad!"

c. Instruct the listener to respond to the statement with an effective listening response. For example, "You resent me telling you what to do."

3. Have the speaker and listener switch roles and continue. This role-play practice session allows the person who is the listener to practice effective speaking and effective listening. The speaker sees the two skills modeled and may gain some insight as to how he or she might respond the next time one of these "expressions of feelings" occurs at home.

IV. HOMEWORK

A. Ask participants to practice effective speaking and effective listening with their children and their spouses during the week.

B. Ask participants to read the guidelines in their workbooks entitled, "How to Conduct a Family Council" (numbered 5C) which will be discussed during Session 6.

C. Collect the FRQs from the participants for use in the next session.

V. EVALUATION OF SESSION 5

Have participants complete the evaluation form for Session 5, numbered 5D.

5A--EFFECTIVE SPEAKING VIGNETTES

Use the following formula to develop a clear message for each situation. "When you _____ (describe the behavior), I feel _____ (use a feeling word) because _____ (tell how the behavior tangibly affected you)."

SITUATION   EFFECTIVE SPEAKING STATEMENT

1. You are frustrated, even a
   bit angry, because your
   fifteen-year-old daughter
   is dawdling, making you
   late for an appointment.

2. Your ten-year-old girl keeps
   postponing going to bed. You
   and your spouse want to discuss
   about private matters, however,
   and your daughter is preventing
   your talk.

3. Your eight-year-old boy has
   borrowed his dad's tools
   without returning them,
   and they were left out in
   the rain.

4. You can't hear yourself think
   while filling out your income
   tax returns because your
   thirteen-year-old son's stereo
   is too loud.

5. You are continually interrupted
   by your four-year-old daughter
   while talking with a neighbor-
   hood guest.

5B--Family Relationships Questionnaire
(FRQ)

Date: _____   Name: _____

The purpose of this exercise is to encourage you to think about your relationships with your spouse, your children, and your stepchildren-- how you get along with each other and what improvements you would like to see made.

A. First, think of your relationship with your children and step-children. Think of situations in which either you or your child have expressed a strong feeling. For example, perhaps your daughter took too long to get ready for bed last night. This made you very angry and you yelled, "If you don't hurry up and get those teeth brushed, I am going to come in there and brush them for you!" Or, perhaps you disappointed your five-year-old son by coming home later than planned and he said, "You don't care about me; you just like to work." Think of five such situations and write below approximately what you or your child said:

1.

2.

3.

4.

5.

B. Now, think about our past discussions on the typical issues and problems for stepparents and their spouses. Also, think about the positive aspects of your relationship. Respond to each item below as openly and honestly as possible. Do <u>not</u> show your answers to anyone, including your spouse. Feel free to use the other side of the page if necessary.

1. In order of importance, list below the three most important things about your relationship that please you now or have in the past.

   1.

   2.

   3.

2. In order of importance, list below three things that you and your spouse disagree about, for example: We do not agree on how to discipline the children.

   1.

   2.

   3.

3. Place either an A, B, or C beside all of the above items in accord with the following guidelines.

   A. You would feel comfortable talking about it with your partner in the group meeting at the present time.

   B. It would be difficult, but not impossible, to talk about it in the group meeting at the present time.

   C. You could not talk about it in the group meeting at the present time.

5C—How to Conduct a Family Council*

Don Dinkmeyer and Gary McKay define a family council as "a regularly scheduled meeting of all family members." This is a special meeting; more than just conversation around the dinner table. It is not a cure-all for family ills but is a way to help unify your family.

The purposes of a family council are to:

1. Discuss the positive things that have happened in the family during the prior week. This gives everyone a chance to note and reinforce the good things family members are doing. Each family member deserves some praise for good behavior or a task well done.

2. Plan family activities. Unless activities are planned in advance, they probably won't happen. By planning in advance, each family member can reserve the "family time" that is agreed on.

3. Discuss and assign household chores. By having a chance to voice their preferences and desires, children are more likely to accomplish their chores and assignments.

4. Discuss family matters, including changes family members would like to see in the family schedule (for example, a different meal time), settling conflicts, and dealing with recurring issues.

---

*"Adapted from Systematic Training for Effective Parenting (STEP): Parent's Handbook. Copyright 1976, by Don Dinkmeyer and Gary McKay. Published by American Guidance Service, Publishers' Building, Circle Pines, MN 55014."
110

5. Allow each family member a chance to be heard; to express his or her opinion, needs, worries, and so on.

Guidelines

1. A family council should last about thirty to sixty minutes.

2. Set a meeting day and time that is agreed upon by _all_ family members. This may require some compromise on the part of several family members.

3. For your first family council, choose an adult as chairperson. Rotate the chairperson position each week thereafter; very young children are exempt. You will also need a recorder; a person who keeps notes of the discussions that are made, chores assigned, and planned activities. Rotate that position also.

The role of chairperson is not to dictate what is discussed or to make final decisions. The chairperson helps keep order by asking for topics of discussion, calling on people to talk as they raise their hands, and so on.

4. Parents and children together should make a list of household chores and then decide who shall do them. By volunteering for some of the less-pleasant chores (for example, emptying the garbage), parents will show the children that they are willing to cooperate and be fair. This does not mean that parents should always be assigned the un-pleasant tasks.

5. Establish a democratic atmosphere by allowing all family members an opportunity to express their views and suggestions. Parents can do

this best by not offering their solutions first. Let the children develop some ideas first--don't jump in too quickly.

6. Do not let the family council become a gripe session. If a person has a complaint, use effective listening and then ask if he or she wants to solve it here in the family council meeting. If he or she does not want to solve the problem, but only complain, remind him or her that complaints are heard in family council only if the complainer is willing to find a solution to the problem.

7. Ask the children to voice matters that concern them. If parents dominate a family council, the children will be "turned off."

8. Agreements made in family council should be put into effect for one week--until the next family council. If a person wants to change a decision, he or she must wait until the next meeting. This way family members will grow to value the family council because that is where family decisions, chore assignments, activities are planned and assigned.

9. Decide on logical and natural consequences that will be applied if a family member fails to do his or her assigned chores. Make these consequences clearly known and understood.

10. Do not spend too much time distributing chores. Otherwise, you will miss planning activities, complementing each other, and sharing concerns. Do not let the meeting evolve into a "job-distribution hour."

Beginning a Family Council

Ask the children if they would like to participate in planning a family activity for the next week. Explain to them that what you are doing is having a family council. Explain the purposes and procedure. During this first meeting, dispense with chore assignments. Work in a discussion of chores, reinforcing each other for positive behaviors, and so on at your second meeting.

Family members who choose not to participate (make participation voluntary) should be told that family decisions are made in family council and if they want a say in how things are going to be, they should attend. Nonattenders will soon begin attending as they see how the family council influences them, too. Be positive and encourage children to participate; but do not force anyone to do so.

Sample Agenda

Your agenda for a family council may include:

1. Reading the minutes of the last meeting.
2. Discussion of old business from last week.
3. Discussion of new business: changes in chore assignments, family fun plans, for example.

Avoid These Mistakes

1. Waiting until every family member wants to participate.
2. Starting late or meeting for too long.
3. Forgetting to take notes.
4. Parents dominating the discussions.
5. Focusing too much on criticisms and mistakes.
6. Forgetting to compliment family members for good behavior.
7. Failing to put plans into action during the next week.

Session 5 Worksheet

5D--EVALUATION OF SESSION 5

Please rate the following items according to how helpful you think they
are/will be to you in your stepfamily situation:

1 = Very helpful

2 = Helpful

3 = Unhelpful

4 = Very unhelpful

_____1. Discussion of last week's homework.

_____2. Discussion of how to make effective-speaking responses.

_____3. Written exercise on using effective speaking.

_____4. Discussion of gearshifting.

_____5. Role playing using effective speaking and gearshifting.

_____6. Practice of speaking, listening, gearshifting.

What was most helpful in this session?

What was least helpful in this session?

How could this session have been more helpful to you?

SESSION 6

I. DISCUSS HOMEWORK

OBJECTIVES: To encourage homework completion by asking for feedback and questions. To assist participants in sharpening their speaking and listening skills.

10 min.
A. Ask each participant to give an example of his or her use of the skills during the past week.

B. Ask for comments on the workbook reading, "Conducting a Family Council." Announce that the group will be discussing the family council in detail during this session.

II. UNIFYING THE FAMILY--THE FAMILY COUNCIL

OBJECTIVES: To teach participants a method of unifying the family--the family council.

20 min.
A. Review the guidelines for conducting a family council (see handout numbered 5C). Ask participants for comments or questions.

20 min.
B. Role play a family council, using the role play directions on Worksheet 6A. You play the role of a parent and choose group members to play the roles of spouse, son, and daughter. Be sure to model the guidelines of the family council, for example, choosing a person to take the minutes, keeping the meeting short, and being democratic.

C. Ask participants for comments or questions regarding the role play.

10 min. BREAK

III. EFFECTIVE PROBLEM SOLVING

OBJECTIVES: To help couples know what to do when effective speaking does not work the first time. To help couples become aware of the effects of using authoritarian or permissive solutions to conflicts. To teach couples a five-step problem-solving method that they can use with each other and with their children.

10 min.

A. Repeating Effective Speaking Statements

"Children, and sometimes your spouse, may respond to your effective speaking statement by ignoring you. This may happen because no one likes to learn that his or her behavior is causing a problem. They may prefer 'not hearing' how their behavior is causing you a problem.

"When this happens we advise you to make another effective speaking statement when the first does not get a response. Perhaps this second statement will come out louder and more intense and will tell the child, 'Look, I really mean it'.

"If, after the second try, the child still ignores you, there are two things you can do. If you determine that there is a conflict of needs between you and the child, use effective problem solving which we will discuss in a moment. Or, if the problem is that the child has failed to follow a family rule or is engaging you in a power struggle, use natural or logical consequences.

116

"A conflict of needs example: Your teenage daughter is about to go out the front door to school. The weather looks threatening and you don't want her to catch a cold by not wearing a jacket. You tell her of your concern, using effective speaking, but she states that her rain jacket is old and it embarrasses her to wear it. This is a conflict of needs: your need to keep her healthy and her need to look good in front of her peers. Effective problem solving is the answer. A possible solution might be the compromise that she carries the jacket in case it rains, rather than wearing it now.

"A failure to follow rules or power struggle example: Your five-year-old son is supposed to take his plate from the table to the sink after dinner--a family rule established in the last family council. You have reminded him, using effective speaking, but he runs outside to play immediately after eating. Use the logical consequence you constructed as a family to handle this situation. He might be ushered back into the kitchen and reminded that: 'We take our plates to the sink before we go out to play'. Keep him in the kitchen until he has followed the rule."

10
min.
B. Present the "Typical Methods of Conflict Resolution," Worksheet 6B. Ask the group members to review it with you and then ask for comments and questions.

C. Effective Problem Solving Steps
    1. Present the five steps in Effective Problem Solving, directing the group members' attention to Worksheet 6C.
        1. Discuss the problem in terms of each person's needs. Stress the use of effective speaking and effective listening during problem solving and especially at this step.

117

2. Brainstorm alternative solutions to the problem. Do
not evaluate any of these solutions at this step--use
your creativity.

3. Evaluate each solution carefully. Which ones are
unrealistic at this time or impossible to implement?
Choose the alternative that both parties agree is best
at this time.

4. Decide how the solution will be implemented. Who will
do what? When? How? By what time, date, and so on? Work
out all the details.

5. Put your solutions to work for a specified period of
time, for example, "We'll try this for a week." Evaluate
how the solution worked and decide on any changes in the
solution or go back to stage 2 again and work through the
remaining stages.

2. Ask for questions or comments about the process. Stress
that problem solving is a method to use with your spouse and
with your children.

10
min.

D. Exercise: Effective Problem Solving
1. Return the Family Relationships Questionnaire that
participants completed in Session 5. Allow five minutes to
review what they wrote and make any additions or corrections.

2. Ask participants to form husband-wife pairs. Instruct
them to discuss their answers to question #2 of Family
Relations Questionnaire (Worksheet 5B), using effective
speaking. Instruct the spouse who is listening to use
effective listening.

118

3. Then ask the couples to discuss their responses to question #3 of the questionnaire and to decide on an issue that they can problem solve. After agreeing on an issue, they are to begin the problem-solving process by discussing the issue using effective speaking and effective listening and gearshifting. They are to only discuss the problem at this time.

IV. HOMEWORK

A. Ask each couple to continue their above discussion at home for at least a twenty-minute period. They are to go no further than step 1 in the process until they feel comfortable that the problem has been defined in terms of each person's needs. They may move on to step 2 at home if possible. No one should proceed past step 2 at this time. Ask couples to decide on a time and place that they will practice. Have each couple report their time and place to the group. This encourages completion of the assignment.

B. Ask participants to review "How to Conduct A Family Council" (Worksheet 5C) and to go over "Effective Problem-Solving Steps" (6C) in their workbooks.

C. Ask each couple to conduct their first family council during the coming week and to bring their comments and questions to the next session.

D. Collect the Family Relationship Questionnaires from partici-pants.

V. EVALUATION OF SESSION 6

Have participants complete the evaluation form for Session 6 (numbered 6D).

6A--Family Council Role Play--Parents

Parents' Roles

We will discuss:

1. Problems with chores at dinner time.
2. Coordination of use of the family car for this weekend.

We will plan a family activity together.

We will compliment the teenagers on:

1. The great job they are doing keeping their rooms clean.
2. Staying home last Sunday night so we could play parlour games together.

We will help our daughter solve her homework problem.

6A--FAMILY COUNCIL ROLE PLAY--DAUGHTER

Situation: You and your parents are going to have your first family council meeting. The idea of a "family council" sounds interesting to you but you are somewhat suspicious. Dad will lead the group and he will ask Mom to take notes. You, as a teenager, will play the role as outlined.

Daughter - Age 13

1. The first item of discussion will be family chores at dinner time. Currently, everyone has a specific job to do--yours is setting the table. Your brother will bring up the fact that he is tired of having to do the dishes. Be cooperative as you discuss this situation with the rest of the family.

2. The second item of discussion will be coordination of the family car this weekend. Be sure to bring up the fact that you need a ride to and from the YWCA on Saturday morning for your swim team practice.

3. The third discussion will be to decide upon a family activity for next week. Make some of your own suggestions.

4. Before the end of the meeting, bring up the problem you are having doing your homework at night. Complain that there is just too much noise--you study at the kitchen table.

6A—Family Council Role Play—Son

Situation: You and your parents are going to have your first family council meeting. The idea of a "family council" sounds interesting to you but you are somewhat suspicious. Dad will lead the group and he will ask Mom to take notes. You, as a teenager, will play the role as outlined below:

Son - Age 17

1. At dinner time at your house everyone has a "chore" to do. Someone sets the table, someone cooks, someone clears the table, and someone washes dishes and loads the dishwasher. For the last two weeks, you have been washing dishes and loading the dishwasher. You are tired of doing it and feel that you have the worst job of all the family members. You will bring up this problem at the family council. As you discuss this issue with the other family members, be cooperative but not passive, stand up for yourself. Cooperate with the group as they attempt to find a better arrangement for everyone.

2. The second item of discussion will be coordination of the family car this weekend. You will need it on Friday night at 8:00 p.m. for a date with Mary Lou.

3. The third discussion item will be a family activity. Make your own suggestions when the family starts discussing this.

6B--Typical Methods of Conflict Resolution

Conflicts in family relationships are almost inevitable. They are not necessarily a sign of weakness or emotional illness. The way conflicts are resolved is the important issue.

There are at least three ways to resolve a conflict. The method chosen will largely determine the kinds of feelings generated in us. Here are three typical methods.

	Method	Who Counts	Resultant Feelings in Me	Resultant Feelings in Others
1.	Authoritarian: "We'll do it my way."	I count. You don't count.	Guilt (later)	Resentment Anger
2.	"O.K. dear, I guess we can do it your way."	You count. I don't count.	Resentment (later) Anger	Guilt
3.	Effective Problem Solving: "Let's find a solution acceptable to both of us."	I count, You count.	Proud Warm Close	Proud Warm Close

6C—Effective Problem-Solving Steps

1. Discuss the problem in terms of each partner's needs. Use effective speaking and listening during problem solving and especially at this step.

2. Brainstorm alternative solutions to the problem. Do <u>not</u> evaluate any of these solutions at this step—use your creativity.

3. Evaluate each solution carefully. Which ones are unrealistic at this time or impossible to implement? Choose the alternative that <u>both</u> parties agree is best at this time.

4. Decide how the solution will be implemented. Who will do what? When? How? By what time, date, and so on. Work out all the details.

5. Put your solution to work for a specified period of time, for example, "We'll try this for a week." Evaluate how the solution worked and decide on any changes in the solution, or go back to step 2 again and work through step 5.

6D--Evaluation of Session 6

Please rate the following items according to how helpful you think
they are/will be to you in your stepfamily situation:

1 = Very helpful

2 = Helpful

3 = Unhelpful

4 = Very unhelpful

____1.   Discussion of last week's homework.

____2.   Discussion of how to hold a family council.

____3.   Role playing a family council.

____4.   Discussion of three typical ways to resolve conflicts.

____5.   Discussion of effective problem-solving method.

____6.   Sharing those things we like about our spouses.

____7.   Practice of problem solving.

What was most helpful in this session?

What was least helpful in this session?

How could this session have been more helpful to you?

SESSION 7

I. DISCUSS HOMEWORK

OBJECTIVES: To encourage homework completion by asking for feedback and questions.

20
min.

A. Discuss with the group their experiences conducting their first family council. Ask for questions, problems encountered, successes, and so on. Use effective listening when participants express either very positive or negative feelings associated with their experience.

B. Review the major concepts and guidelines for having a family council if necessary; the homework for this session will be to conduct another family council.

C. Discuss the participants' experience using the speaking, listening, and problem-solving skills during the past week. Ask for questions.

II. REVIEW: EFFECTIVE PROBLEM SOLVING

OBJECTIVE: To further develop communication and problem-solving skills.

10
min.

A. Review the method discussed last week (see Worksheet 6C). Ask for questions.

B. Distribute the Family Relationship Questionnaires and have the couples review their progress in problem solving on the issue

chosen last week. Their homework assignment was to practice
effective problem solving up through step 2, if possible.

C. Couples are to continue their problem-solving process
beginning with step 2. If they completed step 2 during the week,
have them review step 2 and continue. Observe each couple for
several minutes. Coach and reinforce as necessary, reminding them
to use effective speaking and effective listening.

10
min.
BREAK

D. Couples are to continue the problem-solving process.

10
min.
E. Reassemble participants in the larger group. Ask each couple
about their progress in the problem-solving process, questions or
frustrations.

10
min.
F. At this point, some participants will complain that problem
solving takes too long. This occurs because it is a new skill and
it does take time. However, the time is well spent.

"Reconciling differences is often a time-consuming process.
Simple problems may take only two or three minutes to resolve, but
complicated situations may require several hours to find a suitable
solution. However, this time is well-spent and in the long run
will save much time because no reinforcement is necessary. After
a family member has helped to find a solution and has agreed on
it, there is no need for policing to make certain he or she follows
through. Each participant has an investment in the success of
the solution and can see that his or her needs will be met and
goals achieved if everyone does his or her part. Furthermore, the

128

time spent in resolving differences is constructive interaction. Children receive attention from their parents in a positive way. They are working together as a team to attack a common enemy rather than fighting each other. Further, they are establishing a pattern of communication, making future problem solving less complicated and more efficient. Children learn that parents trust them, and they learn in turn to trust their parents."

III. HOMEWORK

A. Ask the couples to continue practicing effective speaking and effective listening with their children and spouses.

B. Ask the couples to continue their problem-solving process at home during the week. Ask them to spend twenty minutes on the process. Tell them to decide the time and place they will practice now and share their decision with the rest of the group. If a couple has completed problem solving on an issue, tell them to choose another issue and to start working on it at home.

C. Each couple is to conduct their second family council this week. Ask them to write down or tape record what happened, what decisions were made, and how the children reacted.

D. Remind the group that next week is the last session and that they need to think of any other questions they may have so that they can present them next session.

E. Remind group members to bring their Family Relationship Questionnaires to Session 8.

IV. Evaluation of Session 7

Have participants complete the evaluation form for Session 7, numbered 7A.

Please do not put your name
on this questionnaire

7A--Evaluation of Session 7

Please rate the following items according to how helpful you think they
are/will be to you in your stepfamily situation.

1 = Very helpful

2 - Helpful

3 = Unhelpful

4 = Very unhelpful

_____1.   Discussion of last week's homework.

_____2.   Practice of effective problem solving.

_____3.   Discussion of benefits of effective problem solving.

What was <u>most</u> helpful in this session?

What was <u>least</u> helpful in this session?

How could this session have been more helpful to you?

SESSION 8

I. DISCUSS HOMEWORK

OBJECTIVE: To encourage homework completion by asking for feedback and questions.

15
min.

A. Ask each couple to report on their practice of effective speaking and listening during the past week.

B. Do the same for the problem-solving assignment they were given.

C. Ask each couple to report on the results of their second family council. Some participants may not have conducted a family council. Although the family council is not appropriate for every family, most of the group members should know how to conduct one and at least give it a try. Encourage doubtful participants to at least give it a try. The fact that they did not have a family council may be symptomatic of deeper family problems. One of these problems may be that family life is not a priority for them, so they do not plan or make the time in their weekly schedule.

D. Stress to group members that this is the last weekly group meeting, and they should ask any remaining questions they have so they may be answered during this session.

II. EFFECTIVE PROBLEM SOLVING: SKILLS PRACTICE

OBJECTIVES: To further refine communication and problem-solving skills.

132

60 min.   A. Divide the group into husband-wife pairs. Review the problem-solving steps with them (Worksheet 6C). Ask couples to continue the problem solving that they began as homework. If they are ready for a new topic, tell them to select a new issue and begin a discussion beginning with step 1. Observe each couple; reinforce and coach. <u>Note</u>: One hour is available here; it is important that you motivate people to keep practicing.

10 min.   BREAK

III. PROGRAM SUMMARY

OBJECTIVE: To tie all the program components together and review past sessions.

A. Assemble the group and ask for questions and feedback on the problem-solving process. Using effective speaking, let the group know how you feel about the progress they have made in understanding stepparenting and learning the skills presented in the workshop. Say something positive about the skill level and progress of each participant.

10 min.   B. Summarize the content of the program. Ask for questions and comments as you proceed. The emphasis here is on tying the sessions together and showing how the communication skills fit together.

Using your own words and style, cover the following major points in your program summary.

The purposes of the ESP program have been to help participants:

1. Better understand the normal challenges and adjustments in being a stepparent.

2. Better understand the challenges and adjustments that their stepchildren have to make.

3. Share common concerns, problems, joys, and challenges involved in being a stepparent and thereby gain emotional support from the group.

4. Learn a new discipline skill (consequences) that they can use with their stepchildren.

5. Learn communication skills (effective listening and effective speaking) that will enable them to more effectively deal with the emotional aspects of family relationships.

6. Learn how to resolve problems more effectively through effective problem solving.

7. Begin to establish more unity in the family by conducting a family council.

8. Enrich their marriage and understand the importance of a strong marriage to healthy parent-child relationships.

9. In the program we discussed:

    Myths surrounding stepfamilies.

    Typical emotional reactions of children to divorce and remarriage and how to deal with them.

    Adjustment problems for stepparents and their spouses and stepchildren including dealing with discipline, ex-spouses, visitation, finances, and so on.

10. During the first four sessions we learned:

    How to recognize nonverbal communication.

    The barriers to communication.

    How to listen effectively for feelings.

11. During the last four sessions we learned:

How to speak more effectively.

How to gearshift; switching from speaking to listening.

How to apply speaking and listening to problem solving.

12. What else have we learned?

13. What have we not covered that would be useful to you as a stepparent?

15 min.

C. Wrap-up

1. Ask for any other questions or comments.

2. Remind the group of the follow-up session scheduled thirty days from now (see p. 146). Be sure to contact other group members not present on the date, time, and place of the follow-up meeting.

3. Ask group members if they would be interested in a group meeting on the subject of legal matters of concern to stepparents. This type of meeting could be scheduled before the follow-up meeting or as another chance to get together later. Subjects of interest to stepparents are: adoption, custody laws, visitation rights and conditions, wills, medical releases, support payments, ownership of property, choosing a lawyer. Often local attorneys may be willing to speak to the group at no cost. You may want to provide the attorney with a list of the group's questions and concerns prior to the meeting.

If there is interest in such a meeting, make assignments for contacting a lawyer, getting participants' questions to the lawyer, scheduling the meeting, and so on.

135

4. Introduce participants to resources available to step-parents.
    a. Book List for Stepparents--Worksheet 8A.
    b. Book List for Stepchildren--Worksheet 8B.
    c. Resources for Stepfamilies--Worksheet 8C.

IV. HOMEWORK

A. Stress to group members the importance of their continued practice of the communication and problem solving skills. Use the analogy of playing the piano: When you first learn you make a lot of mistakes. Later, you become more polished. But, if you fail to continue to practice, you soon lose the ability to play.

This applies equally to the skills they have learned: They must practice them or lose them. Assign each couple to practice EL, ES, and EPS during the next month with their spouses and children. Tell them they will be asked to demonstrate their skills at the thirty-day follow-up meeting.

B. Assign them to have family council number three and to decide at that meeting how often they will hold a family council in the future weeks.

V. EVALUATION OF SESSION 8

Have participants complete the Session 8 evaluation form, Worksheet 8D.

8A—Book List for Stepparents

Berman, Claire. _Making it as a Stepparent_. New York: Doubleday, 1980.

Dodson, Fitzhugh. _How to Discipline with Love_. New York: Signet Books, 1978.

Duberman, Louise. _Reconstituted Family: A Study of Remarried Couples and Their Children_. New York: Praeger, 1975.

Einstein, Elizabeth. _The Stepfamily: Living, Loving, and Learning_. New York: Macmillan, 1982.

Espinoza, Renata, and Navman, Yvonne. _Stepparenting_. DHEW Publication No. ADM 78-579, U.S. Government Printing Office, Washington, D.C., 1979.

Gardner, Richard. _The Parents' Book About Divorce_. Garden City, N.J.: Doubleday, 1977.

Krantzler, Mel. _Creative Divorce_. New York: Evans & Co., 1974.

Kuzma, Kay. _Part-time Parent_. New York: Wade Publishing, 1980.

Maddox, Brenda. _The Half-Parent_. New York: Evans, 1975.

Noble, June, and Noble, William. _How to Live With Other People's Children_. New York: Hawthorne, 1977.

Ricci, Isolina. _Parenting after Divorce or Remarriage_. New York: Macmillan, 1980.

Rosenbaum, Jean, and Rosenbaum, Veryl. _Stepparenting_. Carte Madera, California: Chandler and Sharp, 1977.

Roosevelt, Ruth, and Lofas, Jeanette. _Living in Step_. New York: Stein & Day, 1976.

Satir, Virginia. _Peoplemaking_. Palo Alto: Science and Behavior Books, 1972.

Visher, Emily B., and Visher, John S. _How to Win as a Stepfamily_. New York: Dembner Books, 1972.

Visher, Emily B., and Visher, John S. Stepfamilies: A Guide to Working with Stepparents and Stepchildren. New York: Brunner/ Mazel, 1979.

Westoff, L. A. The Second Time Around: Remarriage in America. New York: Viking, 1975.

Wald, Esther. The Remarried Family: Challenge and Promise. New York: Family Service Association of America, 1981.

Yours, Mine, and Ours: Tips for stepparents. HEW publication No. (ADM) 78-676, 1978. For a copy, send $1.30 to the Consumer Information Center, Dept. 108A, Pueblo, Colorado 81009.

8B--Book List for Stepchildren

Berger, Terry. <u>A Friend Can Help</u>. Milwaukee: Raintree Editions, 1975.

Conta, Marcia, and Reardon, Maureen. <u>Feelings Between Kids and Parents</u>. Milwaukee: Raintree Editions, 1975.

Eber, Christine E. <u>Just Momma and Me</u>. Chapel Hill, N.C.: Lollipop Power, 1975.

Eichler, Margrit. <u>Martin's Father</u>. Chapel Hill, N.C.: Lollipop Power, 1973.

Gardner, Richard A. <u>The Boys and Girls Book about Divorce</u>. New York: Bantam Books, 1971.

Gardner, Richard A. <u>The Boys and Girls Book About Stepfamilies</u>. New York: Bantam Books, 1982.

Goff, Beth. <u>Where is Daddy? The Story of a Divorce</u>. Boston: Beacon Press, 1979.

Green, Phyllis. <u>A New Mother for Martha</u>. New York: Human Sciences Press, 1978.

Helmering, Doris W. <u>I Have Two Families</u>. Nashville: Abingdon, 1981.

LeShan, Eda. <u>What's Going to Happen to Me? When Parents Separate or Divorce</u>. New York: Four Winds Press, 1978.

Lewis, Helen C. <u>All about Families, The Second Time Around</u>. Atlanta: Peachtree Publishing, 1980.

Sinberg, Janet. <u>Divorce Is a Grown-up Problem</u>. New York: Avon Press, 1978.

Sobol, Harriet L. <u>My Other Mother, My Other Father</u>. New York: McMillan, 1979.

Stenson, Janet S. <u>Now I Have a Stepparent and It's Kind of Confusing</u>. New York: Avon Press, 1979.

8C--RESOURCES FOR STEPFAMILIES*

AUDIOVISUALS

Films

    Stepparenting, New Families, Old Ties - 16 mm, C/S, 25 minutes,
Polymorph Films, 118 South Street, Boston, MA 02111.

        Parents and stepparents of preschool and school-aged children
        discuss some of the problems faced in stepfamilies.

Single Parents and Their Children

Single Parents and Other Adults

Stepparenting Issues

    Each is a series of fourteen separate vignettes designed to
trigger discussion about common problems these families face.
16 mm or video, C/S, 20 minutes, Human Services Department,
116 Soldiers Field Road, Boston, MA 02135.

Filmstrips

    Blended Family. From Families in Crisis, Set 4, Coronet Films,
65 East South Water Street, Chicago, Illinois 60601.

        Describes the problems teenagers had when two families merged.

Dramatizations

    Families - A group of vignettes about the family in various stages
of the life cycle, not specifically stepfamilies.

    Write to: Mrs. Linda Bishop, The Independent Eye, Inc., 115 North
               Arch Street, Lancaster, PA.

    Telephone: 717-393-9088

    Cost: $400 plus certain expenses

---

*This list of resources was prepared in part by Frances J. Wagner,
Extension Specialist, Human Development, North Carolina Agricultural
Extension Service, North Carolina State University, Raleigh, NC 27650.
Used by permission.

<u>Divide and Multiply</u> - A drama about single parents, separation, and divorce.

    Write to: Plays for Living, Family Service America,
                 44 East 23rd St., New York, N.Y. 10010

Newsletters

<u>Remarry-O-Gram</u> - Published by Remarried, Inc.

    Write: Remarried, Inc., Box 742, Santa Ana, California 92701

<u>Stepfamily Bulletin</u> - Published quarterly for the Stepfamily Association of America, Inc. Edited by Elizabeth Einstein, John S. and Emily B. Visher. Includes <u>Kids' Stuff,</u> a section for children.

    Write to: Human Sciences Press, 72 Fifth Avenue, New York,
                 N.Y. 14850

    Cost: $12.00 per year for individuals - $26.00 per year
                 for institutions.

<u>Stepparent News</u> - Published monthly with a combined July/August issue by Listening, Inc., Richard Bennet, ACSE, publisher, Patricia Bennet, R.N., editor. Includes section, <u>Stepping Stones,</u> for children.

    Write to: Listening, Inc., 8716 Pine Avenue, Gary, Indiana
                 46403

<u>Practical Parenting</u> - A bimonthly newsletter by parents for parents, published by Meadowbrook Press, Inc. Executive editor is Vicki Lansky and the associate publisher is Bruce Lansky. Sometimes includes articles of interest to stepparents.

    Write to: Practical Parenting, 15235 Minnetonka Blvd.,
                 Minnetonka, Minnesota 55343.

    Cost: $5.00 for six issues (one year); $9.00 for twelve
                 issues (2 years).

Bumper Stickers

Since public education is important, the distribution of bumper stickers may help make the public more aware of stepparents and their needs.

STEPPARENTS TRY HARDER   Order from Human Development Department, Box 5097, N.C. State University Raleigh, N.C. 27650 Cost: 50¢ each

HAVE YOU HUGGED YOUR STEPMOTHER TODAY?   Order from Stepfamily Association of California, Inc., 900 Welch Road Suite 400 Palo Alto, CA 94394 Cost: $1.50

Tee-Shirts

Write to: Step-Shirts, Box 14D, 322 W. 72nd St., New York, N.Y. 10023

Style 1: WICKED STEPPARENT ("Wicked" struck out and heart encircles "stepparent") $12.50 each.

Style 2: Depicts a kangaroo carrying a panda bear in her pouch, $12.50 each.

Note: Specify sex, size, and style.

Organizations

AFACT, P.O. Box 1428, Phoenix, AZ 85001. Association for Fathers and Children Together, nonprofit, twenty-four-hour hotline (602) 956-7999. Provides lawyer referral, hotline, emotional support.

Equal Rights For Fathers. Jack Hutslar, Chairman, P.O. Box 117, High Point, NC 27261 (919) 784-4926.

<u>Remarrieds, Inc.</u>, P.O. Box 742, Santa Ana, CA 92701. "To be eligible for membership one must be married and either formerly married, or married to a previously married person, or must have been separated and reunited." Local chapters may be formed by ten or more couples who apply for charter from the national organization. Chapter Formation Kit is available for $2.00. Contact: Bill Alexander, Rt. 2, Box 874A, Monroe, N.C. 28110.

<u>Local family service agencies</u> affiliated with Family Service America, 44 East 23rd Street, New York, NY 10010.

<u>The Stepfamily Association of America, Inc.</u>, 900 Welch Road, Suite 400, Palo Alto, CA 94304. A nonprofit educational organization; acts as a support network and national advocate for services for stepfamilies. The association provides for local chapter meetings, mutual help groups and stepfamily discussion courses. It also offers public educational programs and professional workshops.

Why Have An Organization?

A stepfamily is a unique kind of family which, like all families, needs education and support. Stepparenting is different from parenting, being a remarried parent is different from being a parent in a first marriage family, and growing up in a stepfamily can be more complicated than growing up in a biological family. Because there are specific challenges faced by stepfamilies which are not addressed by existing community services, Stepfamily Association of America, Inc. acts as a support network and national advocate for services for stepparents, stepchildren and remarried parents.

8D--Evaluation of Session 8

Please rate the following items according to how helpful you think they are or will be to you in your stepfamily situation.

1 = Very helpful

2 = Helpful

3 = Unhelpful

4 = Very unhelpful

_____1.   Discussion of last week's homework.

_____2.   Practice of effective problem solving.

_____3.   Summary of the program.

_____4.   Discussion of future meetings and subject matter.

What was most helpful in this session?

What was least helpful in this session?

How could this session have been more helpful to you?

7

THE THIRTY-DAY FOLLOW-UP MEETING

PURPOSES

The purposes of the thirty-day follow-up meeting are:

1. To provide a refresher in communication skills training.

2. To get feedback on how group members have been applying the information and skills taught in the program in their family lives.

3. To encourage the establishment of a formal or informal support group for stepparents that can meet as often as the group decided.

4. To answer questions about the content of the program and its application in the family setting. The purpose of the homework assignments is to help participants generalize the skills to the family setting.

5. To determine current and future needs of stepparents.

RECOMMENDATIONS

1. Hold the follow-up meeting in the home of a group member (a volunteer, of course).

2. Make arrangements for light refreshments.

3. Make the meeting half social and half skills practice. You can use role-play examples from the program manual or invent new

ones. Have members practice effective speaking and listening. Ask them to list in order the steps in problem solving. Ask them how to conduct a family council.

Ask them any other questions you think are appropriate.

4. Make meeting short and fun, the recommended meeting length is two hours.

BIBLIOGRAPHY

Anderson, James O., Larson, Jeffry H., and Morgan, Ann. "The Parenting Program for Stepparent Families: A New Approach For Strengthening Families," in Family Strengths 3: Roots of Well-Being, ed. Nick Stinnett, et al. Lincoln, Nebraska: University of Nebraska Press, 1981.

Becker, Wesley. Parents Are Teachers. Champaign, Ill.: Research Press, 1971.

Bitterman, Catherine M. "The Multimarriage Family." Social Casework, 49 (1968): 218-21.

Dinkmeyer, Don C., and McKay, Gary. Systematic Training for Effective Parenting (STEP): Parents' Handbook. Circle Pines, Minn.: American Guidance Service, 1976.

Fast, Irene, and Cain, Albert C. "The Stepparent Role: Potential for Disturbances in Family Functioning." American Journal of Orthopsychiatry, 36 (1966): 485-91.

Flack, F. F. A New Marriage: A New Life. New York: McGraw-Hill, 1978.

Glick, Paul C. "A Demographer Looks at American Families." Journal of Marriage and the Family, 37 (1975): 15-26.

Gardner, Richard. The Parents' Book about Divorce. New York: Doubleday, 1977.

Goldstein. H. S. "Reconstituted Families: The Second Marriage and its Children." Psychiatric Quarterly, 48 (1974): 433-40.

Gordon, Thomas. Parent Effectiveness Training. New York: Wyden, 1970.

Guerney, Bernard. Relationship Enhancement. San Francisco: Jossey-Bass, 1977.

Gurman, Alan S., and Kniskern, David P. "Research on Marital and
Family Therapy: Progress, Perspective and Prospect." In S. L.
Garfield and A. E. Bergin (eds.), Handbook of Psychotherapy and
Behavior Change: An Empirical Analysis. 2d ed. New York:
Wiley, 1980.

Jackson, D. "The Eternal Triangle." In Jay Haley and Lois Hoffman
(eds.), Techniques of Family Therapy. New York: Basic Books,
1967.

Kompara, Diane R. "Difficulties In the Socialization Process of
Stepparenting." Family Relations, 29 (1980): 69-73.

Kleinman, Judith, Rosenberg, Elinor and Whiteside, Mary. "Common
Developmental Tasks in Forming Reconstituted Families." Journal
of Marital and Family Therapy, 2 (1979): 79-88.

Leslie, Gerald R., and Leslie, Elizabeth M. Marriage in a Changing
World. New York: Wiley, 1977.

Lofas, Jeanette. "Discipline and Structuring--Crucial Problems for
Stepfamilies." Marriage and Divorce Today, 5 (1980): 3-4.

Maddox, Brenda. The Half-Parent. New York: Evans, 1975.

Mayleas, D. Re-Wedded Bliss: Love, Alimony, Incest, Ex-spouse and
other Domestic Blessings. New York: Basic Books, 1977.

Messinger, Lillian. "Remarriage Between Divorced Persons with Children
from Previous Marriage." Journal of Marriage and Family Counseling,
2 (1976): 193-200.

Messinger, Lillian, Walker, Kenneth N., and Freeman, Stanley J.
"Preparation for Remarriage Following Divorce: The use of group
techniques." American Journal of Orthopsychiatry, 48 (1978):
263-72.

Miller, Sherod, Nunnally, E. W., and Wackman, D. B. Couple Communication Instructor Manual. Minneapolis, Minn.: Interpersonal
Communication Programs, Inc., 1977.

148

Morgan, Ann. "The Development of Stepfamilies: An Examination of Change Within the First Two Years." Ph.D. diss., Texas Tech University, 1980.

Mowatt, M. H. "Group Psychotherapy for Stepfathers and Their Wives." Psychotherapy: Theory, Research, and Practice, 9 (1972): 328-31.

Nichols, W. C. "Today's Major Clinical Issue: The Remarried Family." Marriage and Divorce Today, 5 (1979): 2.

Perkins, T. E. "Natural-Parent Family System Versus Stepparent Family System." Ph.D. diss., University of Southern California, 1978.

Rallings, E. M. "The Special Role of Stepfather." The Family Coordinator, 25 (1976): 445-49.

Reingold, C. B. Remarriage. New York: Harper & Row, 1976.

Roosevelt, Ruth, and Lofas, Jeanette. Living in Step. New York: Stein & Day, 1976.

Rosenbaum, Jean and Rosenbaum, Veryl. Stepparenting. Carte Madera, Calif.: Chandler & Sharp, 1977.

Satir, Virginia. Conjoint Family Therapy, 2nd ed. Palo Alto: Science and Behavior Books, 1967.

Simon, A. W. Stepchild in the Family. New York: Odyssey Press, 1964.

Stern, P. N. "Stepfather Families: Integration Around Child Discipline." Issues in Mental Health Nursing, 1 (1978): 50-56.

Visher, Emily B. and Visher, John S. "Common Problems of Stepparents and their Spouses." American Journal of Orthopsychiatry, 48 (1978): 252-62.

_____. Stepfamilies: A Guide to Working with Stepparents and Stepchildren. New York: Brunner/Mazel, 1979.

Waldron, J. A. and Whittington, R. "The Stepparent/Stepfamily." Journal of Operational Psychiatry, 10 (1979): 47-50.

Wald, Esther. _The Remarried Family: Challenge and Promise_. New
     York: Family Service Association of America, 1981.
Walker, Kenneth N., Rogers, Joy, and Messinger, Lillian. "Remarriage
     After Divorce: A Review." _Social Casework_, 58 (1977): 276-85.